Marietta Holley

Twayne's United States Authors Series

Nancy A. Walker, Editor
Vanderbilt University

TUSAS 658

MARIETTA HOLLEY
Frontispiece from Samantha at Saratoga, 1887. Courtesy of Jane Curry.

Marietta Holley

Jane Curry

Twayne Publishers
An Imprint of Simon & Schuster Macmillan
New York

Prentice Hall International
London • Mexico City • New Delhi • Singapore • Sydney • Toronto

Twayne's United States Authors Series No. 658

Marietta Holley
Jane Curry

Copyright © 1996 by Twayne Publishers
All rights reserved. No part of this book may be reproduced or transmitted in any form or by any means, electronic or mechanical, including photocopying, recording, or by any information storage and retrieval system, without permission in writing from the Publisher.

Library of Congress Cataloging-in-Publication Data

Curry, Jane, 1945–
    Marietta Holley / by Jane Curry.
       p. cm. — (Twayne's United States authors series ; TUSAS 658)
    Includes bibliographical references (p.) and index.
    ISBN 0-8057-4020-1 (acid-free paper)
    1. Holley, Marietta, 1836–1926—Criticism and interpretation.
I. Title. II. Series.
PS1949.H5Z6 1996
813'.4—dc20   95-8678
                                                                                    CIP

The paper used in this publication meets the minimum requirements of American National Standard for Information Sciences—Permanence of Paper for Printed Library Materials. ANSI Z39.48–1984. ∞ ™

10 9 8 7 6 5 4 3 2 1 (hc)

Printed in the United States of America

In joyful memory of my witty grandmother
Mary Knight Curry

Contents

Preface ix
Chronology xi
Introduction xiii

> *Chapter One*
> Marietta Holley and Josiah Allen's Wife   1
>
> *Chapter Two*
> Soaring Into Eloquence for Wimmen's Rites:
> *My Opinions and Betsey Bobbet's*   12
>
> *Chapter Three*
> Gentility and the Sentimental Tradition:
> *Samantha at Saratoga, or, Flirtin' with Fashion*   31
>
> *Chapter Four*
> Upholding Duty's Apron Strings:
> Temperance, Race, and Religion   40
>
> *Chapter Five*
> Etcetery, Etcetery, Etcetery:
> The Later Works   68
>
> *Chapter Six*
> Writ Down by Males, and Translated by 'Em Mostly   81

Notes and References   95
Selected Bibliography   107
Index   111

Frontispiece from Samantha Among the Brethren.
Courtesy of Jane Curry.

Preface
(Which It Is Necessary to Read)

Marietta Holley's literary persona "Samantha Allen" adored prefaces and would no doubt feel bereft if a book about her creator's work should leave port without one. In fact, Holley's commingling of author and persona is sometimes articulated, in dialect form of course, in prefaces ostensibly written by "Josiah Allen's Wife" of Jonesville but signed by her in "Bonney View," near Adams, New York—Holley's home. In the preface to *Sweet Cicely, or, Josiah Allen as a Politician*, Josiah refers to Cicely as one of Samantha's "thought-children," a term often used by Holley to describe her books. Samantha claims to love sweet Cicely better than any of her other thought-children, even though it isn't right to think more of one child than another. Thus the literary character Samantha acknowledges her authorship of the literary character Cicely when of course Holley created them both. Then when the book begins, Cicely is a real person who visits her "creator" Samantha. As the river pilot announced to the steamboat passengers when they approached Cairo Point, "Ladies and Gentlemen, just ahead is the confusion of the Ohio and Mississippi Rivers."

I understand this "confusion" of Holley, Samantha, and Holley/Samantha's characters. Because I have performed as Samantha for a number of years, she walks around with me, uttering the occasional "tejus" or "dubersome" or "tuckerin'" when I least expect it. People have often asked whether I have any difficulty keeping myself separate from this delightful alterego. I don't have any trouble, I say, but you'd have to ask her if she does.

Marietta Holley, who so ardently argued through Samantha for adjustments in the separate spheres ideology and proclaimed the right and need for women to engage the public sphere, herself preferred the quiet home life. Her thought-children spoke in public for her. Publishing in each of five decades between 1873 and 1914, she eventually produced a brood of more than 20 books, which have served as the primary sources for this study.

Through her "middlin' dry" wit, Holley's Samantha favored common sense and "megumness" as the "2 cords to cling to" in life as she "soared into eloquence" for social justice. "Speakin' in a poeticule way," as Holley's characters were wont to do, it is particularly fitting that this volume on Marietta Holley, tireless advocate for woman suffrage, is being published during the seventy-fifth anniversary of the Nineteenth Amendment to the U.S. Constitution.

Jane Curry
Minneapolis, Minnesota

Chronology

1836   Marietta Holley born 16 July in southern Jefferson County, New York, seventh and youngest child of John and Mary (Taber) Holley.

1850   Brothers Jerome Brightman, Dewitt, and John Holley, Jr., leave home to go west.

1857   First prose story, "Piety," published in *Jefferson County Journal*.

1861   Father dies.

1869   July, short story published in *Peterson's Magazine*, first use of pseudonym "Josiah Allen's Wife."

1873   *My Opinions and Betsey Bobbet's*.

1877   *Josiah Allen's Wife as a P. A. and P. I.: Samantha at the Centennial*. Mother dies.

1880   *My Wayward Pardner, or, My Trials with Josiah, America, the Widow Bump, and Etcetery*; *The Lament of the Mormon Wife*; *Betsey Bobbet: A Drama*. Mentor and publisher Elisha Bliss dies.

1881   Travels outside Jefferson County for first time.

1882   Attends opening of Neil Burgess play, *Betsey Bobbet*, in Providence, Rhode Island.

1883   *Miss Richards' Boy and Other Stories*.

1885   *Sweet Cicely, or, Josiah Allen as a Politician*.

1887   *Samantha at Saratoga, or, Flirtin' with Fashion*; *Miss Jones's Quilting and Other Stories*; *Poems*. Invited to the White House by President and Mrs. Grover Cleveland. Meets Clara Barton, who was to become a close friend.

1888   Has 15-room Victorian home built near family farmhouse and calls it Bonnie View.

1890   *Samantha Among the Brethren*.

1892   *Samantha on the Race Problem*, republished 1894 as *Samantha Among the Colored Folks*.

1893 *Samantha at the World's Fair.* Eight-year-old May Shaver comes to Bonnie View as unofficially adopted daughter.
1895 *Samantha in Europe.*
1904 *Samantha at the St. Louis Exposition.* May Shaver marries and leaves Bonnie View.
1905 *Around the World with Josiah Allen's Wife* (had been serialized in 1899).
1906 *Samantha vs. Josiah, Being the Story of a Borrowed Automobile and What Came of It.*
1909 *Samantha on Children's Rights.*
1911 *Samantha at Coney Island and a Thousand Other Islands.*
1913 *Samantha on the Woman Question.*
1914 *Josiah on the Woman Question.*
1915 Sister Sylphina, with whom Holley has lived all her life, dies.
1926 1 March, Holley dies at home, probably of cancer.
1931 "The Story of My Life," published posthumously and serially in the *Watertown Daily Times.*

Introduction

In her own time, Marietta Holley was a famous American literary humorist. The evidence to support this claim is abundant. An unnamed writer in the January 1905 *The Critic* said of her: "Miss Marietta Holley has done much to add to the gaiety of nations. As 'Josiah Allen's Wife,' she has entertained as large an audience, I should say, as has been entertained by the humor of Mark Twain."[1] In *The Wit of Women*, an 1885 anthology compiled specifically to demonstrate that indeed women had (and should have) a sense of humor, Kate Sanborn asserts that Holley "has caused a tidal wave of laughter by her 'Josiah Allen's Wife' series."[2] In fact, Sanborn offers only a brief quotation from Holley in the anthology because "Samantha Allen" was already "a family friend from Mexico to Alaska" (69). And, in *Horse Sense in American Humor*, Walter Blair claimed that Samantha, rustic philosopher farm wife of wit and gumption, was "one of the most popular characters in American humor, male or female."[3]

Various biographical sketches likewise proclaimed Holley's popularity: "'Josiah Allen's Wife' was a household word for many years"[4]; she "has written some of the most mirth-provoking books that have ever been given to the public"[5]; "[Miss Holley's] readers are scattered over the entire world and include men and women of every station and grade."[6]

"Betsey Bobbet" Clubs formed throughout the country for the purpose of reading together and acting out parts from Holley's books. A dramatization by professional actor Neil Burgess was an ongoing success for several seasons in the 1880s in Boston and New York City.[7] Holley commanded fees as high as $14,000 for a single book. Her books sold hundreds of thousands of copies and were translated into several languages.

Like many famous people, Holley received numerous unsolicited requests. She was asked to "sell aprons at distant fairs, have [her] photograph on sale; shingle churches, lift mortgages, buy homes for various strangers for various reasons, and publish poems and prose books."[8] She was asked to endorse "extra fine" brands of soap, "equally excellent" breakfast food, and even patented medicines. Sacrificing financial opportunity but remaining true to her retiring nature, she declined these invitations. Those enticements, however, offer yet another indication of the extent of Holley's renown. She was a star, a "household name." Had she lived in late twentieth-century America, she might have graced the literary equivalent of the Wheaties cereal box.

Yet, unlike Mark Twain, to whom she was compared, Marietta Holley has been largely forgotten until recent years when her work has been revisited and revived, primarily by feminist scholars.[9] Her omission from standard works on American literature and humor, however, is not a slight peculiar to Holley.[10] Women writers have often been ignored altogether or relegated to a footnote in critical studies of American literary humor. The course of Holley's individual literary reputation will be discussed in chapter 6. But before turning to the specifics of her life and works, it is important to place Holley in the context of both the vernacular tradition and the women's tradition of humor in nineteenth-century American literature.

The most engaging form of humor for the nineteenth-century American reading public was delivered via the vernacular or dialect language. In *Women Vernacular Humorists in Nineteenth-Century America: Ann Stephens, Frances Whitcher, and Marietta Holley*, Linda Morris claims that this tradition, which emerged in the Northeast and Southwest in the 1830s, has been particularly important because "it was the first humor that was distinctively American in its language and attitudes, because of its influence on the work of Mark Twain, and because it was the forerunner of American literary realism."[11] In secondary accounts and anthologies of primary sources, literary critics have generally divided nineteenth-century American humor into three categories: Down East, Southwest, and the Literary Comedians. Some authors cite the Local Colorists as a separate branch. The vernacular was critical to all of them.

Vernacular or dialect humor was rendered in the language of the common person who eschewed the lofty syntax and vocabulary of standard English in favor of more familiar, down-to-earth idioms, generally conveyed through creative misspellings, extensive homey metaphors, and the insights of the wise innocent. These heroes and heroines were often uneducated, but were blessed with healthy doses of "horse sense" and mother-wit.[12] They applied their observations of life (experienced often but not exclusively in a rural setting), to local, national, and even international topics ranging from sewing circles to the U.S. Congress in Washington to the Spanish-American War. The authority commanded by their genuine and ingenuous natures exposed various forms of foolishness and absurdity, hypocrisy and fraud, injustice and double standards.

The colloquial language was inextricably tied to the values it articulated. Speakers bore witness to the changing American landscape of social, political, and cultural norms, to the dichotomy between rural and urban, vernacular and genteel.

Among the innovations of the early vernacular prose humorists, particularly Seba Smith (creator of the Maine farm lad Jack Downing in the 1830s) and Frances Whitcher (creator of the Widow Bedott in the 1850s) from the Down East tradition, was the development of first-person narrators. As Linda Morris explains in her critical account of Whitcher's work: "Many humorists of the nineteenth century wrote from a third-person point of view, but first-person vernacular humor ultimately had the greatest long-term appeal to generations of readers . . . . No standard narrator stood between the reader and the vernacular character; no one else was present to interpret the action, or even to comment on it; instead, vernacular characters spoke in their own voices, they represented their own points of view, and they spoke directly to the reader. Their foolishness, their eccentricities, and their common sense all grew out of their characterizations."[13]

Most of the writers were men and much of the subject matter centered on generally masculine concerns and pursuits. Down East humor often featured the exploits of Yankee peddlers and political observers set against the solid background of New England village life and values. In the Southwest humor tradition, stories abound with accounts of hunting trips, gambling, courtships and weddings, fights, horse trades and races, shooting matches, political life, travel, frontier medicine, and the like.[14] It was a humor characterized by raw energy, exuberance, exaggeration, earthiness, and boldness of physical movement in a territory offering independence.

Some of the literary comedians writing in the last half of the century, such as Peter Finley Dunne, reflected the urbanization and industrialization that converged to forge a new face for America. Dunne's "Mr. Dooley," an Irish saloon keeper in Chicago who offered his observations in dialect on every conceivable topic of current interest, was essentially an ethnic cracker-box philosopher of the city, one who plied his listener patrons with opinions and spirits in a setting socially unsuitable for women.

In fact, most of these activities lay outside the realm of women's direct experience. As Morris summarizes, ". . . by and large much of the vigor and the energy of vernacular humor derives from the relative mobility and activity of men in nineteenth-century American society"

(*Vernacular*, 18). Women were not totally absent, but their depiction was often negative, if not downright demeaning: "Again and again, American humorists endow their female characters with thoroughly undesirable qualities. Woman is nearly always one or more of the following: vain, scolding, capricious, coquettish, unpredictable, curious, impractical, loquacious, gullible, muddle-headed, gossipy, gushing, back-biting, jealous or vindictive. Woman's wagging tongue seldom rests and petticoat government via the 'curtain-lecture' rarely abates."[15]

Women vernacular humorists, on the other hand, used many of the same ingredients of the tradition, but baked a different cake. They used dialect, malapropisms, cacography, and extended metaphors. They assaulted sentimental literature and genteel society. They commented on current events and topical issues. They exposed the incongruity between official mythology and the reality of daily lives. But what anchored the observations of their characters was not the mobility and activity afforded to men in the society, but rather the rich details of domestic life. Huck Finn could always "light out for the territories," but female protagonists sought the "fixed environment of home."[16]

Marietta Holley built especially on the earlier work of Frances Whitcher in creating a strong female protagonist who spoke in the first person using a dramatic monologue form. In the 1840s and 1850s Whitcher had created three distinctive female personae—Permilly Ruggles, Aunt Maguire, and the Widow Bedott. Through Permilly she burlesqued the sentimental tradition; with Aunt Maguire she modeled a strong woman of sound reason and common sense as a vehicle for satire. And in her best-known persona, the Widow Bedott, Whitcher created a comic fool whose unremitting husband-hunting and revelations of small-town happenings became the talk of real-life communities whose members angrily fancied themselves the models for Whitcher's unflattering characterizations.[17]

Unlike Holley, Whitcher was no feminist. The Widow Bedott in fact embodied many of the unappealing characteristics attributed to women by many male vernacular humorists.[18] But in Whitcher, Holley had a literary sister who, as Morris suggests, "exposed the hypocrisy that accompanied widespread scrambling for social status" and offered a critique of "women's diminished role in society, especially the way women demeaned themselves and one another" (*Gentility*, 8).

In the first book-length study of the female tradition in American humor, *A Very Serious Thing: Women's Humor and American Culture*, Nancy Walker takes her title from the observation by Frances Whitcher that "it is a very serious thing to be a funny woman." Walker maintains that the common themes of women's humorous expression have indeed been rooted in their subordinate status within the male-dominated culture. The theme of "women's desire to claim autonomy and power"—as expressed in both overt and covert texts—is central to American women's humor. Like women writers generally, women humorists have needed to be taken seriously as intellectually capable people who, like men, can perceive absurdity and convey it to others. "Women's humor is an index to women's roles and values, and particularly to their relationship with American cultural realities. Being a female humorist in America has been problematic in a number of ways that are tied closely to other issues in women's history: the tension between intellect and femininity, male and female 'separate spheres,' women's status as a minority group, and the transforming power of a feminist vision."[19]

In exploring the relationships between cultural realities and women's humorous responses to them, Walker concludes that the central problem of the female humorist in America has been "the fact that humor is at odds with the conventional definition of ideal womanhood. Humor is aggressive; women are passive. The humorist occupies a position of superiority; women are inferior" (12). Female humorists by necessity explore the delicate balance between power and powerlessness. They employ familiar stereotypes—the nag, the scolding wife, the man-chasing spinster, the gossip, the inept housekeeper—but the purpose is often to mock the stereotypes by showing their absurdity and even their danger. Walker continues, "Embedded in the humorous writing of American women for more than 150 years is an exploration of powerlessness that constitutes a subversive protest against it" (10).

Women humorists have not typically taken as their subjects or forms the frontier tall tales and political satires. Instead, they have turned to domestic topics of housework, community affairs, children, and relationships between men and women. Walker observes that from overtly feminist humor to the "housewife" humor of the 1940s and 1950s, the texts call into question the gender-based assumptions and norms of our culture and, particularly in the case of satire, call for a corrective. "By presenting the *results* of women's cultural conditioning and subordination, America's female humorists implicitly address the *sources* of women's self-doubt, dependence, and isolation from the mainstream of American life" (30).

Marietta Holley's overtly feminist humor speaks directly to such issues as economic dependence, lack of political power, double standards, and outright discrimination. She was grounded in the most popular male humor tradition of the nineteenth century; she was one of the most important and successful foremothers of the women's humor tradition; and she was committed to the primary agendas of the women's rights movement. She offered a rustic farm wife character at a time when the mother-wit style was increasingly anachronistic. She mastered the conventions of the beloved vernacular tradition and then transformed them, confronting the gender values of the dominant culture and subverting them. She turned the addled malapropism of Benjamin Shillaber's Mrs. Partington into an elucidation of social criticism when spoken by Samantha. For example, when Samantha referred to the female "sect" instead of female "sex," she was not merely misstating for mirthful purposes. As Morris has shown, she was underscoring a sense of "otherness": "True, we laugh for a moment at Samantha's mistake, but its primary function is to call attention to a society that has tried to turn a whole sex into a quasi-religious cult. Likewise, when Samantha Allen refers to woman's 'spear' rather than her 'sphere,' her author alerts us that in her writings she is going to insist that women's relegation to the private sphere be transformed into a weapon for social change" (*Vernacular*, 8).

Nineteenth-century women humorists routinely attacked the assumptions of the genteel society that valued the image of women as properly idle, helpless, isolated, obsessed with material goods and social status, and dependent on men for their economic survival. But, according to Morris, it would not be "until 1873 with the publication of Marietta Holley's first humor book that a woman humorist would focus on the relationship between sentimentality, the genteel ideology, and the women's rights movement" (125). Through Samantha, Holley offered clear alternatives that she hoped would lead to realizing women's political equality with men and achieving women's full human potential.

Chapter One

Marietta Holley and Josiah Allen's Wife

Family, Childhood, and Youth

Born 16 July 1836 on the family farm in southern Jefferson County in upstate New York, Marietta Holley was the last of seven children born to John Milton and Mary Taber Holley. Of English ancestry, the Holleys claimed descent from the famous astronomer, Edmund Halley. Marietta's grandfather, David Holley, supported the American side during the Revolution and was rewarded with government bounty land. After the war, he moved with his wife Sarah and three generations of his family from Connecticut to the woodlands of northwestern New York, clearing the land for farming and building a cabin for shelter.[1]

David's son John Milton subsequently enlisted in the War of 1812, returning at age 33 and marrying Mary Taber, daughter of Justice of the Peace Lemuel Taber and Sarah Brightman Taber of Bear Creek, in 1817.[2] On their wedding day, John and Mary Holley moved into the frame cottage he had built on a parcel of the Holley homestead outside of Pierrepont Manor given him by his father. Marietta Holley would live on that same parcel for her entire life.

Mary Holley bore four sons and three daughters, the eldest son dying in infancy. Born when her mother was 40, Marietta was the youngest by eight years. A small, frail child, she suffered an inordinate shyness exacerbated by a lisp and the merciless teasing of her brothers. As she grew older, she participated with her mother and sisters in the routine daily and seasonal work on the farm: tending the garden, doing housework, canning, cooking, sewing, quilting, and so forth. Like her eventual character Samantha, Marietta Holley knitted mittens to trade for goods at the general store and was well-versed in the barter economy that valued apples, eggs, butter, and woolen socks as currency for exchange.[3]

In her leisure, she occupied herself with continuous "scribbling" on any scrap of paper she could find. Her father's discarded cash books, account ledgers, even the back of surplus wallpaper became the canvas for her verses, rhymes, and drawings. Even after she became a famous, financially secure author, Holley continued to hoard precious paper, writing a journal in old proof copies of *My Opinions and Betsey Bobbet's* and using an 1852–53 copy of *Patent Office Report* for a scrapbook.[4]

Despite the scoffing of brothers that prompted her to hide her "crude scribblings" and blush with "shrinking timidity," the young Marietta Holley nourished a desire to be a writer. As she remembered from the perspective of old age: "Though money was always scarce and we lived in the simplest way, we were never in want for the necessities of life, and I had abundant time and leisure for reading, scribbling and drawing pictures, which was my great recreation at that time, for I meant to be a great artist."[5]

Marietta's education took several forms. Her formal education at the district school ended when she was 14, about the time her brothers left home to head west and her efforts were needed to supplement the family income. Though reading matter at home was scarce, the supper table was often the site of lively discussions about religion and politics, especially the various reform movements of the day. In matters of religion, the Holleys had traditionally favored the Episcopal Church. Marietta's father John, however, became a Universalist. When she was 16, Marietta joined the Baptist Church after her conversion at a revival meeting. Significantly, women in the Baptist Church were given the right to vote in church matters and the opportunity to participate fully in all Baptist meetings except formal Sunday services.[6]

In politics, family members believed in the cause of both abolition and temperance but debated the specific strategies to those ends.[7] Even when she didn't have the price of admission, Marietta was able to read accounts in the local paper of the lectures on temperance, abolition, suffrage, phrenology, spiritualism, and other topics given by Lyceum speakers booked at the nearby opera house.[8] A "highly educated" neighbor woman gave young Marietta informal, private lessons in botany and other studies.[9] In her posthumously published autobiography, "The Story of My Life," she describes her youthful approach to learning:

> I had a passion for learning everything, but not through hard work and steady application. I did not like that, but gleaning every bit of knowledge that I could that came easily. Astronomy, botany, French, drawing—all had their turn, passionately followed for a time, and filling my waking moments. . . . I was wont to scribble verses when I should have

been trying to master the multiplication table (an instrument of vague torture to my mind) and fill any blank pages with faces more or less resembling the human countenance. As my dresses grew longer so did my scribblings increase.[10]

It was, however, while attending the district school that Marietta observed what was to be one of the most telling lessons of her life education. A local schoolteacher who boarded around with various families became an example to the obviously talented Marietta of an independent woman willing to risk community disapproval in order to fulfill her dreams and potential. The teacher left the school to become a traveling book agent and wrote a book describing her experience.[11] Then she went back out on the road to sell her own book. For many in the neighborhood, this behavior was not respectable in a woman; she was considered "forward." But Marietta admired her. The idea that she knew someone who had written a book and sold it made a lasting impression on her.[12]

This nameless woman with the "slight, erect figure and plain, determined face" also influenced Marietta with her belief in spiritualism and her concern with diet and health. Throughout her life Marietta believed in the possibility of direct communication with the spirit world and searched for contact through such vehicles as Ouija boards, automatic writing, and mediums. And the frail child grew into a woman whose daily regimen included "eating, dressing, and exercising conscientiously, even fastidiously."[13] As an adult, she continued to suffer recurrent respiratory illnesses and chronic pain in her writing hand. But her cautions apparently paid off—she lived to be nearly 90 years old.

In 1861 John Holley died, leaving a household that now included only Marietta, her mother, and her sister Sylphina. Sylphina was a ghostly presence in the house she never left, quickly rustling out of sight when unexpected visitors arrived. The family simply said she was "peculiar from birth." A married sister, Angeline, lived on a nearby farm. The Holley women lived together in that house and the subsequent one Marietta built with later earnings on an adjacent plot until each in turn died. They relied on themselves and whatever day labor they could arrange to keep the house in order and derive income from the farm.

Early on Marietta was able to contribute to the family economy in a way that was acceptable for an unmarried woman by engaging another of her passions—music. She had learned to play the piano through the generosity of an uncle who paid for her lessons. Eventually, she became proficient enough to accept students herself, buy a melodeon on which to give lessons, and bring in much-needed cash. She continued giving lessons even as she published poems and short pieces in magazines, until finally, with the publication of her first book, her income was derived from writing alone.

In her autobiography, Marietta is not forthcoming about courtships in her youth. She acknowledges that there were suitors, and even proposals of marriage, but reveals no details of name or circumstance:

> Heaven only knows why I never married. I only know that when the situation became imminent, and got to the stage of "take me or leave me," it was always easier for me to take the latter course. But my heart was touched sometimes and my feelings lacerated, but yet more than once with the tears in my eyes I was able to turn my back on care and matrimony. . . . The wave of attraction . . . turned the other way and washed me high and dry on the shore of Celibacy.
>
> There are many reasons that conspire to clip the wings of Cupid, a perhaps overstrained sense of duty to those dependent in a way for support and companionship and the inborn love of freedom that rebels at being bound by even Love's golden chains are some. . . . And Art is a jealous mistress and one who follows her would do well to weigh the question well before setting up another rival.[14]

She also said, in an intriguing entwinement with her literary persona, that "Josiah needed her." She may indeed have found the state of "single blessedness"[15] more suitable to both her personal and creative needs. Unlike the fictional spinster she would create, Betsey Bobbet, Marietta saw no humiliation in her unmarried state and seems to have made a conscious choice in the matter. And, as her biographer Kate Winter has speculated, "For a personality as timid and private as hers, the intimacy of marriage must have seemed indeed threatening."[16] Whatever the young Marietta's ambivalence may have been, she was clearly committed to her mother, her sister, her home, and her art.

The Early Years

After composing verses practically since the time she could first read and write, Marietta Holley first saw her words in print when she was 21 years old. Two poems, "Welcome to Summer" and "Phair and Phalse," were published in the 23 July 1857 issue of the *Jefferson County Journal* under the pen name Jemyma. In the second chapter of her autobiography Holley remembers: "Heavens knows why I took that plebeian name, unless it was a revolt at the fancy names, the Jenny Junes, the Minnie Myrtles, and Fanny Ferns." In 1903 she told an interviewer, Mabel Wagnalls: "I recognize how inappropriate such youthful names become as writers grow old. With this in mind I first wrote under the name of 'Jemima,' [sic] which I felt was plain enough and strong enough to sail on triumphant to 90, if need be."[17] In keeping with her intense need for privacy, her reticence, and her fear of ridicule if rejected, Marietta had told no one about submitting the poems and did not declare herself even to her family until she knew they praised the poems without knowing the kinship of their author.

In the next issue of the *Jefferson County Journal* Holley's first prose sketch, entitled "Piety," was published. Though it was written in "good English," here in nascent form were the seeds of her later success with the Samantha books. As Winter describes it: "In a single piece Holley addressed many of the subjects she would continue to wrestle with for the next sixty years: the vanity of fashion, work over worship, the value of class status, the absurdity of the 'cult of true womanhood,' the evils of drink, and the importance of staying close to the land. At the same time she had found her most effective mode: a single strong female voice speaks against one or two other—usually contrary—voices in a rather static situation" (27).

As her confidence grew, Holley sought the counsel and criticism of established poets of the day, among them Mrs. L. H. Sigourney and Oliver Wendell Holmes. Both offered encouragement, if not exactly glowing praise. Mrs. Sigourney wrote that Holley undoubtedly had "the gift of poetical powers" and Holmes noted that her poems showed "a practical talent . . . which may by cultivation produce good fruit."[18] As it happens, Holley's poems were in fact all too similar to the kinds of poems she satirized in her later books. Were it not for the advice of her cousin Henry Holley, maudlin death poems and odes to nature in the sentimental style of the day might have been Holley's legacy.[19] And not even the most eager graduate student would have resurrected her work on their account.

Henry Holley advised his cousin Marietta to write stories instead of poems and essays. Though she considered poetry and standard English the more valid literary forms, she followed his advice and built her reputation on her "dialect sketches." With the publication of "Fourth of July in Jonesville" in the July 1869 issue of *Peterson's Magazine*, her vernacular character and new pseudonym, Josiah Allen's Wife, made their first appearance.[20] In an interview with Mabel Wagnalls, Holley explained why she had chosen this nom de plume:

> ... I became possessed with the idea of writing something wherein I endowed principles with personality. To absolute practicality I gave the name "Samantha," and to the opposite principle of weak sentimentality I gave the name "Betsy Bobbit" [sic]. All my other characters sort of grew up around these two. "Samantha," as I said, was altogether practical, but she knew that love is the greatest thing in the world, so she loved and married "Josiah," and while lacking in sentiment her love was nevertheless so solid that she was willing to take second place before all the world as plain "Josiah Allen's Wife." (61)

Of course, by claiming authorship by a woman without her own name and defined only by her affiliative status with a man, Holley cannily disarmed critics hostile to her feminist aims. In "The Story of My Life" she claims not to remember why she chose the "homely patronymic." She does speculate that she "might have thought any arguments would be received more graciously and it would soften somewhat the edge of unwelcome arguments to have the writer meekly claim to be the wife of Josiah Allen and so stand in the shadow of a man's personality" (Ch. 4).

At any rate, *Peterson's Magazine* published the first story she sent them and everything she offered from then on. Holley never lacked for a publisher again.

Her ambition went beyond the magazines of the day, however. She wrote to Elisha Bliss, president of the American Publishing Company, whose authors included Mark Twain, Brett Harte, Josh Billings, and Charles Dudley Warner. She sent Bliss a poem, a selection from a sentimental story called "Gypsy and I" previously published in 1872 in the *New York Home Journal*, and for contrast a sketch in dialect by "Josiah Allen's Wife." Boldly, she asked whether he would like her to write a book for him. To her delight, he answered immediately: yes, begin at once. To her dismay, he wanted the dialect Samantha. Despite her entreaties that the other work held more literary merit and a Samantha book would be a "dead failure" and "none would ever want to read it," Bliss held firm in his conviction that "Josiah Allen's Wife" could reach a new and immense public.[21]

With the publication of *My Opinions and Betsey Bobbet's* in 1873, the pinched economic existence of the Holley women was eased. The many tasks Marietta had performed to bring in money were consolidated, for the rest of her career, into the discipline of writing. At age 37, Marietta had emulated her former schoolteacher by writing a book. Ironically, her book was sold around the country by subscription, introduced into rural homestead, village, town, and city by traveling book agents very much like the one Marietta had so admired.

The Middle Years

Marietta had told no one but her mother and sister Sylphina that she was writing *My Opinions*. Once it was published, the secret was out and the reaction among surprised neighbors was likened to "a loud clap of thunder bursting forth from a teacup."[22] *My Opinions* was well-received by the public, with at least five American editions published the first year and an edition in London by Routledge and Sons. Portions of the book were serialized in the *Home Journal*. Josiah Allen's Wife was on her way to becoming a household name. As she would for the balance of her writing career, Holley continued to write for the magazines, often in the sentimental prose style she favored over the popular dialect sketches. To these pieces she signed her own name.

Elisha Bliss commissioned another book from America's newest horse-sense humorist, this one capitalizing on the 1876 centennial of the nation's independence. Refusing to travel outside the confines of her immediate North Country environs, Marietta wrote about the Centennial Exposition at Philadelphia relying entirely on maps, photos, guidebooks, and descriptions. She followed this pattern with nearly all her later "travel" books. With the exception of Saratoga Springs and Coney Island, she never visited any of the places before she wrote about them, preferring instead to write her narratives without the encumbrance of directly perceived reality.

Marietta's mother had been her protector, advocate of her special talents, and confidante from childhood. In 1877, shortly before publication of Holley's second book, *Josiah Allen's Wife as a P. A. and P. I.: Samantha at the Centennial*, Mary Holley died of pneumonia.[23] The household that once had numbered eight was now reduced to the two unmarried sisters. And three years later, in 1880, her publisher Elisha Bliss, whom she had grown to depend on as a mentor and friend, also died. That same year she helped organize and fund a circulating library in the town of Adams and published *My Wayward Pardner*, the long poem *The Lament of the Mormon Wife* and *Betsey Bobbet: A Drama*.

Her world had begun to widen somewhat in the 1870s when she attended Lyceum lectures at the Cooper Opera House and entertainments offered by such members of society as businessman General Solon Hungerford of the neighboring town of Adams. At these gatherings she met such people as Henry Ward Beecher, Bayard Taylor, Wendell Phillips, General Sherman, Frederick Douglass, Vice-President Schuyler Colfax, Reverend Antoinette Brown, and Susan B. Anthony.[24] Elisha Bliss had wanted to introduce her to the literati in Hartford (home of Samuel Clemens, Harriet Beecher Stowe, Charles Dudley Warner, and others), but Holley preferred the seclusion of her rural life, receiving visitors but eschewing travel.

Her reputation as a humorist and reformer established, she was sought out by other champions of social justice to publicly assist their causes. In 1877 Frances Willard invited her to be a delegate to the annual convention of the Women's Christian Temperance Union in Chicago. In 1878 Susan B. Anthony urged her to attend the convention of the National Woman Suffrage Association and later, in 1886, appealed to her to address the U.S. Congress. Despite the many entreaties urging her to the podium, Holley followed what she felt was her true nature, which rendered her "unfitted for public life."[25] She did not attend the conventions and never gave a public speech. Her connections with political allies were maintained primarily by correspondence, which became a lively conduit of information and shared views that often made their way into her books in folksy form. Anthony sent her the Congressional Election Committee's report against the suffrage amendment petitions with the quip, "Samantha may have a comment to make on it."[26] Over the years, Willard, Anthony, temperance advocate U.S. Senator Henry Blair, and others sent pamphlets, tracts, trial transcripts, congressional proceedings, and speeches.

Not until 1881, at age 45, did Holley venture for the first time outside her insular world of the farm, Pierrepont Manor, Adams, and nearby Watertown. She finally accepted an invitation from the persistent Dr. Alonso Flack, president of Claverack College on the banks of the Hudson River, for an extended visit with him and his wife. Subsequently, in 1885, she began making yearly visits to New York City, staying at the Murray Hill Hotel, writing, seeing her publishers, attending readings and receptions, and meeting friends. Over the years, she traveled to Washington, D.C.; Virginia; and Chicago, met many of the prominent people of the day including two presidents and four first ladies, and visited for weeks at a time with newfound friends. Though still living in the country, Holley was no longer the obscure country woman. Unlike her character Samantha, who journeyed to New York City in her "best alpacy," Holley wore silks and brocades. In 1903 Mabel Wagnalls described her: "So much has been said and written about the resemblance of Marietta Holley to her own creation "Samantha" that some erroneous impressions have been received. "Samantha," it is true, expresses Miss Holley in many ways; her principles are firm as rock and her sense of humor is abounding and abiding; but in appearance and culture Miss Holley is more like a Grand Duchess than the homely character she has immortalized. Her spectacles are a pair of gold lorgnettes, her gowns are made by a French modiste, and she has no need of a cap" (61).

Among her expanding circle of friends were Will Carleton, a popular humorist and author of *Farm Ballads*, and his wife as well as Bishop and Mrs. John C. Newman. In 1887 she was invited to the White House to meet President and Mrs. Grover Cleveland. On that same visit to Washington, D.C., she met Clara Barton, founder of the American Red Cross, who was to become one of her closest friends until Barton's death in 1912.

By the 1880s, her success occasioned so many requests from publishers of magazines and weeklies that she could not oblige them all. The editor of the *Yankee Blade* offered her $500 for a four-page story.[27] Besides the aforementioned works published in 1880, during the decade she published *Miss Richards' Boy* (1883), *Sweet Cicely, or, Josiah as a Politician* (1885), *Samantha at Saratoga* (1887), and *Poems* (1887). And she was becoming a shrewd businesswoman, securing ever more money as she negotiated her own book contracts. For *My Opinions* she was paid $600. For *Samantha at Saratoga*, which was to become her best-selling book and a better seller for the entire decade of the 1880s,[28] Holley asked for and received $10,000. Later, for *Samantha at the World's Fair* (1893), she commanded $14,000.[29]

Though she visited and traveled more than she once could have imagined, Holley still preferred the quiet home life, where from the window in her writing room she could see the woods, plants, flowers, and streams of nature. With financial comfort now ensured, she decided to have a house built to replace the small cottage to which her mother had been brought as a bride. A 15-room Victorian house, constructed on the homestead and later called "Bonnie View," was finished in 1888. In addition to Marietta and Sylphina, the household now included a handyman, Lew Hoxie, who would be employed for nearly 20 years, as well as a housekeeper. In her new study at "Bonnie View" she wrote her works on the church and race, *Samantha Among the Brethren* (1890) and *Samantha on the Race Problem* (1892), and the nearly dozen books that would follow.

In addition to her periodic bouts with pneumonia and bronchitis, Holley was hampered by severe pain in her writing hand. Before *Samantha at the World's Fair* she had customarily written in longhand the outline and two complete drafts of books that often numbered 500 to 600 pages in print. At the suggestion of a clergyman writing to wish her well, with *Samantha at the World's Fair* she began a pattern wherein she penned the outline of a book and then dictated into a phonograph. Lew Hoxie learned to type and transcribed the text. Later, having mastered Samantha's dialect, Hoxie typed directly from the rough sketch. Even after he left his full-time employment with Holley, he continued to type her manuscripts until the last one, *Josiah Allen on the Woman Question* (1914), was sent to the publishers.[30]

The rhythms of Holley's life now included her writing, her visitors, her charities, her yearly excursions to New York City, and her love of nature. Into this ordered existence came a child. At age 58, Holley took in May Shaver, the eight-year-old daughter of the subscription book agent for *My Wayward Pardner*. Though she never legally adopted May, Holley treated her as a daughter, rearing and educating her until she left home to marry. Holley had referred to her fictional characters as her thought-children. Kate Winter notes:

> To another woman writer she wrote a congratulatory note on the emergence of her "mind-child." Later, when she visited the writer at her home, Holley was amazed, wondering "how can she ever write her bright books in this place, for her three pretty children, little flyaways, seemed to be everywhere present. No spot seemed to be exempt from their noisy and riotous presence." Writing and motherhood appeared to be incompatible to Holley. Books were peaceful, long-lived progeny. Even Clara Barton recognized that the books were a substitute for a brood of offspring. In a letter praising *Samantha at the World's Fair*, Clara exclaimed: "What treasures your 11 children are; what a family to sit honoringly on your shelves, and look lovingly upon you, as you create for them still another companion." (120)

When Clara Barton was leaving for a Red Cross relief mission in Turkey, Holley sent her a gift for the crossing: "my latest child, *Samantha in Europe*." Now there was a flesh-and-blood child in her home, and, though she continued writing, for a few years Holley was more preoccupied with Bonnie View and May. After *Samantha in Europe* in 1895, she did not publish another book until *Samantha at the St. Louis Exposition* in 1904.

Into the New Century

In her later works she continued to engage the "woman question" as well as temperance, children's rights, peace and justice, poverty, conflict between capital and labor, and even imperialism. With the exception of an occasional gem that puts a folksy, horse-sense slant on a current event in the early twentieth century culture, however, these books are endlessly repetitious and generally lackluster. She borrows wholesale from earlier works, sometimes lifting entire chapters with only a change in the character's name.[31] Too often the moralizing and sentimentality of these narratives remind us of what her writing might have been like without her keen sense of wit and humor.

In 1914, at age 78, Holley published her last book. And like her first one, it centered on women's rights. Despite its other shortcomings, *Josiah Allen on the Woman Question* is unique in Holley's body of work: it is the only one in which Josiah, not Samantha, is the narrator. After 40 years of "curtain lectures" and "eppisodin,'" the debate between Samantha and Josiah continued, Samantha's right to vote still unwon.

In 1915 Holley's sister Sylphina died. May had married and left home. Marietta's lifelong bouts with illness continued sporadically, and an elevator between the first and second floors was installed in Bonnie View. Her last writing was an autobiography to be published serially in the *Watertown Daily Times* after her death. In what is a generally disappointing and deliberately vague memoir, she omits any useful chronology and important dates (for example, she doesn't happen to mention what year she was born) and skirts much that would be self-revelatory. She had championed both suffrage and temperance when they were unpopular causes in Jefferson County and elsewhere. She lived to see both the Eighteenth and Nineteenth Amendments added to the U.S. Constitution. Yet we do not know whether Marietta Holley voted. Her literary persona had argued for suffrage for four decades, so it would be reasonable to expect an account of that dramatic event in Holley's life, but if she did vote, she leaves no description of it.

Despite her many illnesses and infirmities, Holley remained handsome and relatively active in her old age. In fact, no one including her relatives knew how old she was when she died in her room at Bonnie View on 1 March 1926. As she had said of her first down-to-earth pseudonym, she had "sailed on triumphant" to nearly 90. When the North Country ground had thawed in late spring, she was buried in the cemetery next to the Episcopal Church in Pierrepont Manor.

Chapter Two
Soaring into Eloquence for Wimmen's Rites: *My Opinions and Betsey Bobbet's*

In her first published book, *My Opinions and Betsey Bobbet's* (1873), Marietta Holley introduces her favorite theme of "wimmen's rites" as well as the main characters and literary devices that would advance that theme in the coming decades. The inordinately long subtitle of the book signals the intended audience: "Designed as a Beacon Light, to guide women to life liberty and the pursuit of happiness, but which may be read by members of the sterner sect, without injury to themselves or the book." Written under the pseudonym Josiah Allen's Wife, *My Opinions* is dedicated to "My own Lawful Pardner, Josiah. Whom (although I have been his Consort for a little upwards of 14 years) I still love with a cast-iron devotedness." Marietta Holley and Samantha Allen are thereby conjoined, not to be fully separated until Holley's name finally superseded her character's on the title page of her penultimate book, *Samantha on the Woman Question*, 40 years later in 1913.

In the preface, Samantha places her interest in "wimmen's rites" within the context of another major social issue of her day—abolition. She had favored abolition, "the subject of black African slavery also wearin' on me" for some time, and turned her thoughts to writing on the "woman question" only after emancipation. Though the idea of writing a book "kept a goarin'" her, Samantha hesitated because she wasn't schooled in grammar and spelling. In addition, she had not had access to experiences of adventure that would make a book interesting: "I cant write a book, I don't know no underground dungeons, I haint acquainted with no haunted houses, I never see a hero suspended over a abyss by his galluses, I never beheld a heroine swoon away, I never see a Injun tommy hawked, nor a ghost; I never had any of these advantages; I cant write a book."

Josiah, for his part, had offered his special brand of encouragement: "But who will read the book Samantha when it is rote?" Ever "clost with his money," Josiah proclaims that he will not pay one cent to hire anybody to read it.

Thus, before the first page of narrative in the book, Holley has established the vernacular nature of her character, ensured Samantha's status as a devoted wife and Josiah's as the penurious husband, and mocked the sentimental and gothic adventure fiction of the period.

The first two chapters of *My Opinions* reinforce Samantha's standing as a wife bound by the pure light of love to her "lawful pardner," a good stepmother to his children, a practical farm woman of 204 pounds heft whose cooking, gardening, and housekeeping are second to none (though she says it who shouldn't). She is possessed of endless good judgment and is adept at "moral eppisodin'." Though she protests both categories, she is also immodest and ceaselessly talkative. Thomas Jefferson and Tirzah Ann, Josiah's children by his former "relict," live with them in a one-and-a-half-story yellow house on a 75-acre farm that's "all paid for." They have good barns, an orchard, bee hives, and a meadow sweet with the smell of clover in the summer.

Samantha declares that they "are about as happy as the most of folks." With classic understatement, she does however warn others of her "sect" who find themselves in the "tryin' place" of second consorts by virtue of marrying a widower: "if the relict goes to comparin' you to his foregone consort, *don't encourage him in it.* On this short rule hangs the hope of domestick harmony" (20; emphasis in original).

Though she isn't "high learnt," this unschooled rustic claims acquaintance with the classics through Thomas Jefferson, who read them to her by the fire while he pursued his studies. Holley's wide reading is reflected in the many authors and works Samantha alludes to throughout the course of the books she pens; to wit: Milton's *Paradise Lost*, Pollock's *Course of Time*, Shakespeare, Dante, Dickens, Ruskin, Homer, Euripides, Sophocles, Thackeray, German poets Schiller and Goethe, and "Mr. Plato's" dialogues, among others. She often cites the Bible and *Foxe's Book of Martyrs* and magazines such as *Peterson's*, *Harper's Bazar*, and *Atlantic Monthly*.

A foolish foil, Josiah is naturally vain, proud, and egotistical. A lightweight both as "measured by the steelyards" and as measured by intelligence, this 100-pound bald weakling displays tendencies toward sentimental foolishness and impractical schemes that Samantha is repeatedly obliged to break off. A devoted "pardner" but incapable of exercising common sense and good judgment, he doggedly presents the often incongruous masculine argument that would keep women strictly in the private sphere.

The topic of "wimmen's rites" is introduced via Betsey Bobbet, the man-chasing spinster who "haint handsome . . . and don't seem to be contented." The extended physical description of Betsey places her character squarely among the standard stereotypes of comedy. With her skinny frame, bad complexion, large nose, bald head, false teeth, and frizzled wig, she is not "in good order." But unlike other authors who simply made fun of the ugly old maid, Holley offers the image of a love-hungry spinster made ridiculous precisely because she has accepted the prevailing sex-role norms. The problem is not Betsey Bobbet the individual, but the dearth of culturally endorsed alternatives to marriage for women in a society that boasts of opportunity for all.

Betsey represents the genteel ideal taken to its logical extreme. Just as her attempts to enhance her appearance are all artificial, Betsey's aspirations to gentility are likewise false and an affront to common sense. Betsey, who describes herself as an "ahdent sole" whose feelings have to gush out in poetry ere she "expiah," "talks dreadful polite and proper." Her greatest weakness in Samantha's eyes is that she is "dretful" sentimental. "I have seen a good many that had it bad, but of all the sentimental creeters I ever did see Betsey Bobbet is the sentimentalest, you couldn't squeeze a laugh out of her with a cheeze press" (27).

Samantha, on the other hand, proclaims: "Sentiment ain't my style, and I abhor all kinds of shams and deceitfulness." She sees "feelins that stalk round in public in mournin' weeds" as shallow, surface posturing that has nothing to do with genuine emotion. Through Betsey, Holley satirizes the conventions of sentimental poetry, the genteel tradition, and the notion that separate gender spheres relegate women to the role of clinging vine.

Betsey, like the forever mournful Emmeline Grangerford in Mark Twain's *The Adventures of Huckleberry Finn*, is always right on the spot with a poem, generally one that rhapsodizes for 25 verses or so. She writes her "gushin's of a tendah sole" for the two local papers, *The Gimlet* or *The Augur*, depending on whichever one of the editors is more recently "widowered." To wit, three verses from her poem "A Song":

> Not for strong minded wimmen,
> Do I now tune up my liah;
> Oh, not for them would I kin-
> dle up the sacred fiah.
> Oh, modest, bashful female,

> For you I tune up my lay;
> Although strong minded wimmen sneah,
> We'll conqueh in the fray.
> Chorus.—Press onward, do not feah, sistehs,
> Press onward, do not feah;
> Remembeh wimmen's speah, sistehs,
> Remembeh wimmen's speah.
>
> . . . .
>
> Yes, wedlock is our only hope,
> All o'er this mighty nation;
> Men are brought up to other trades,
> But this is our vocation.
> Oh, not for sense or love, ask we;
> We ask not to be courted,
> Our watch-word is to married be,
> That we may be supported.
> Chorus.—Press onward, do not feah, sistehs, etc.
>
> . . . .
>
> Oh, do not be discouraged, when
> You find your hopes brought down;
> And when you meet unwilling men,
> Heed not their gloomy frown;
> Yield not to wild dispaih;
> Press on and give no quartah,
> In battle all is faih;
> We'll win for we had orteh.
> Chorus.—Press onward, do not feah, sistehs,
> Press onward, do not feah;
> Remembeh wimmen's speah, sistehs,
> Remembeh wimmen's speah. (184–85)

Betsey is a woman against women's rights. She proclaims in her affected speech that "wimmen's only speah is to marry." Like Josiah, she believes that women's rightful place is as nurturer in the home, a poultice soothing the lacerations of the manly breast torn by life's cares. It is not in the public sphere exercising the franchise to vote. For her part, though she thinks smiling and cooing would do a woman just as much good as it does a man, Samantha maintains that she would be willing to coo—if only she had the time. While doing at least four chores simultaneously, a perspiring, overextended Samantha rejects this sentimental stereotype. "'Am I a poultice Betsey Bobbet, do I look like one? . . . What has my sect done' says I, as I wildly rubbed [Josiah's] shirt sleeves, 'That they have got to be lacerator soothers, when they have got everything else under the sun to do?'" (62).

Samantha argues that true marriage is born of independence. The idea of marrying a man for a home or out of fear of being called an *old maid* is reprehensible. Women wouldn't do that if they could support themselves and "be thought as respectable for 'em to earn *their* livin' as for a man to." If they could achieve economic self-sufficiency and societal respect on their own, women would marry for the only reason that makes marriage pure and holy—love.

Holley, in fact, compares economic marriage to prostitution. At the end of the novel, when Betsey has finally snared the hapless Simon Slimpsey and attained the status of a married woman, Samantha accuses women who marry without love of selling themselves, swapping their purity, their self-respect, and their soul with the "minister for salesman": "Nor I don't want these wimmen that have sold themselves for a certificate with a man's name on it. . . . What have they done different from these other bad wimmen, only they have got a stiddy place, and a little better wages, such as respectability in the eyes of fools and etcetery" (417).

Woman's sphere, says Samantha, is where she can do the most good. As she says in *Samantha Among the Brethren*, "If God had meant wimmen to be nothin' but men's shadders, He would have made gosts and fantoms of 'em at once. But havin' made 'em flesh and blood, with braens and souls, I believe He meant 'em to be used to the best advantage."

In *My Opinions* Holley establishes the structure and the literary conventions she would return to again and again in the next four decades. *My Opinions* is a loosely connected narrative told in the first person by a rustic philosopher blessed with endless reserves of horse sense. The dialect humor derives from the vernacular language itself, malapropisms, and the collision of Samantha's deadpan, pragmatic logic with the flowery conventions of her various foils. Though Betsey Bobbet is featured in only one more book, *Josiah Allen's Wife as a P. A. and P. I.: Samantha at the Centennial* (1877), and a play, *Betsey Bobbet: A Drama* (1880), Josiah serves Holley throughout the body of her work as the foolish spokesman for the status quo.

Lengthy descriptions of domestic chores, local happenings, customs, and mores often consume entire chapters between those devoted more particularly to arguing an idea. For example, there are chapters describing the donation party for the minister, the deceptions of a charming peddler, Josiah's off-key warbling with the choir, a young suitor with accordian serenading under the wrong window, the dreaded surprise parties foisted on unwilling hosts, all days' visitings, and so forth. These particularities of domestic and community life, both those sanctioned and those satirized by Holley, provide a rich, daily, rural context within which to posit ideas that reach far beyond the local confines of Jonesville.

As she would do in her later books, Holley uses real figures and events for her fictional characters to interact with and react to. Samantha meets many of these people as she travels away from Jonesville, braving the perils beyond the safety and comfort of home in order to "soar into eloquence" for the Cause of Right. Samantha approaches the mightiest politicians—President Ulysses S. Grant and presidential hopeful Horace Greeley—as if they are neighbors who seek her good counsel. She thinks of Queen Victoria of England as the "Widder Albert," thus simultaneously bringing her to the level of "just folks" and embracing her as a woman, one who has lost her husband and mourns as Samantha would for Josiah. Samantha meets luminaries of the women's rights movement—Elizabeth Cady Stanton, Susan B. Anthony, Dr. Mary Walker, and Victoria Woodhull—as well as fictional types such as a women's rights lecturer. She offers both admiration and admonition, as appropriate to Samantha's "megum" (medium) views.

An advocate of the primary agendas of the women's rights movement begun at the Seneca Falls, New York, gathering in 1848, Holley gives personality via her characters to the predominant pro- and anti-suffrage arguments discussed in Aileen Kraditor's book *The Ideas of Woman Suffrage, 1890–1920*. The two major prosuffrage arguments were based on justice and on expediency, respectively. Thus, Samantha argues for equality of the sexes because it is a natural human right, but she advocates the vote primarily as a means to justice and social purity. Holley accepts the concept of women as moral and cultural guardians and argues for enfranchisement as an avenue toward protecting home and children. The four standard arguments—biological, theological, sociological, and sentimental—made by antisuffragists find folksy articulation in Betsey, Josiah, and numerous other "antis" who populate the Samantha books.[1]

When Samantha travels outside of Jonesville, she takes on the age-old mantle of the "wise innocent," the country observer of unfamiliar places, people, and values. A long line of American humorists have used this technique—among them Seba Smith in *The Downing Papers* and Mark Twain in *The Adventures of Huckleberry Finn*. Jack Downing travels from his home in Maine to observe the state legislature and eventually to advise President Andrew Jackson. The insights of this "country bumpkin" outsider, as revealed in his letters home, expose the hypocrisy, corruption, and pretensions of urban life and politics. Twain's Huck Finn is a wise innocent by virtue of his age; he is a child who offers a straightforward, honest account of what he sees in his travels, generally with no judgment implied. The adult reader, on the other hand, knows that these observations in fact puncture the various conventions (notions of chivalry, genteel sentimentality, slavery, and so on) they describe.

Holley's Samantha, like Benjamin Shillaber's more muddled Mrs. Partington, is prone to multiple malapropisms. When Samantha journeys to New York City, she thinks the train conductor, who merely wanted to collect her ticket, is being forward by offering his hand. When a man asks her "Will you have a bus mom?," she interprets the offer of transportation as a request for a kiss. She replies with moral indignation born of ignorance and misunderstanding:

> If that man had the privilege of livin' several hundred years, he would say at the last 100, that he never forgot the look I gave him as he uttered these infamous words to me.... I told him plainly, "That if I wasn't a married women [sic] and a Methodist, and, was free to kiss who I was a mind to, I had jest as lives kiss a anacondy, or a boyconstructor, as him," and I says in conclusion, "mebby you think because Josiah haint here to protect me, you can talk to me as you are a mind to. But, says I, "if I haint got Josiah with me I have got a good stout umberell." (290)

Onlookers who recognize her mistake are bemused; Samantha is self-satisfied at having set the culprit straight. While these embarrassments of vocabulary are meant to be humorous, they serve to point up Samantha's foibles. However, when her indignation is aimed at a worthy target—a foolish foil, a wrong-thinking politician, an injustice—Samantha's wisdom often scores a bull's-eye via imagery rich with domestic metaphor.

Holley's technique is to allow a foil to advance a point of ideology. Samantha then reduces ideology to a concrete image, renders that image ridiculous when set against the reality of women's daily lives, and thereby calls into question the validity of the ideology. For example, both Josiah and Betsey profess the ideology of separate gender spheres. Men belong in the public sphere; women in the private sphere. Women's only "spear" is to marry; her role is to coo, cling, and soothe. Samantha makes tangible the clinging vine and applies it to Betsey's case.

> She has tried to make a vine of herself to all kinds of trees, straight and crooked, sound and rotten, young and old. Her mind is sot the most now, on the Editer of the Augur, but she pays attention to any and every single man that comes in her way. And it seems strange to me that them that preach up this doctrine of woman's only spear, don't admire one who carries it out to its full extent. It seems kinder ungrateful in 'em, to think that when Betsey is so willin' to be a vine, they will not be a tree; but they won't, they seem sot against it. I say if men insist on makin' runnin' vines of wimmen, they ought to provide trees for 'em to run up on. . . ." (133–34)

In a later book, *Samantha at the St. Louis Exposition* (1904), Holley uses this same technique to challenge one of the premiere images of Victorian genteel womanhood: woman on a pedestal. Josiah suggests that women are "cooin' doves" and "seraphimes" and God's own angels brought down to earth. And they "ort" to be "riz up" on a pedestal. Samantha takes that image literally, reminds him of her 204-pound heft, and conjures the unlikely vision of her getting up and down off a pedestal, only periodically perched because the children need lookin' after, the dinner needs to be cooked, there's moppin', mendin', churnin' to be done, "etcetery." Her conclusion? It's too "tuckerin'" to be on a pedestal.

Through Samantha, Holley notes the repetitive, unending nature of women's work, as well as the need to juggle several projects at one time. She laces Samantha's descriptions of women's daily lives with rich recitations of daily chores and domestic detail. The sheer volume of those chores as well as the strength, stamina, and planning required to perform them belies the notion that women are too "fraguile and delikate" to go to the poll.

When Josiah offers that rationale, Samantha plays on the word "poll" and speaks with "witherin' dignity and self respect":

> There is one pole you are willin' enough I should go to, Josiah Allen, and that is the hop pole . . . you think that for a woman to stand up straight on her feet, under a blazin' sun, and lift both her arms above her head, and pick seven bushels of hops, mingled with worms and spiders, into a

gigantic box, day in, and day out, is awful healthy, so strengthenin' and stimulatin' to wimmin, but when it comes to droppin' a little slip of clean paper into a small seven by nine box, once a year in a shady room, you are afraid it is goin' to break down a woman's constitution to once. (92)

Women are likewise enfranchised to handle the cistern pole, and Samantha guesses that "the political pole wouldn't draw much harder than that does." She leaves Josiah momentarily speechless when she yet again points out the dichotomy between the genteel ideal of women as "lacerator soothers" and the practical reality of women's lives: "You may go into any neighborhood you please, and if there is a family in it, where the wife has to set up leeches, make soap, cut her own kindlin' wood, build fires in winter, set up stove-pipes, dround kittens, hang out clothes lines, cord beds, cut up pork, skin calves, and hatchel flax with a baby lashed to her side—I haint afraid to bet you a ten cent bill, that that womans husband thinks that wimmin are too feeble and delicate to go to the pole" (93).

As she would do many times in subsequent books, Holley underscores the irony of the disenfranchisement of half the population in a country whose founding patriots had resisted taxation without representation. Samantha reserves particular disdain for the "large, healthy lookin'" orator at a Fourth of July picnic who uses the podium of freedom's celebration to rail against women's rights with all the usual arguments about delicacy, modesty, and weakness: "Why, before he had got half through, a stranger from another world who had never seen a woman, wouldn't have had the least idee that they was made of clay as man was, but would have thought they was made of some thin gauze, liable at any minute to blow away, and that man's only employment was to stand and watch 'em, for fear some zephyr would get the advantage of 'em" (167). Voting would be too much hardship to foist upon these "seraphines." Just then, Samantha comes upon the man's bedraggled wife, who arrives just as he concludes his remarks. She is exhausted from doing all her own chores plus his and walking three miles carrying three children. Her husband couldn't help her because he "had to make a great exertion today, and he wanted to have his mind free and clear." The irony of the occasion is obvious, the ideas of the speaker are totally at odds with even his own domestic reality, and the wife is collaborating in her own oppression by praising "how beautiful he can talk."

Samantha's forthright announcement in the preface that the theme of the book is "wimmen's rites" presages an episodic narrative that ranges within that theme from suffrage to sentimentality, temperance to free love, the double standard to fashion. She advocates equal pay for equal labor, a mother's equal right to her children, and the right to speak out in public without being considered "unwomanly." She undermines arguments claiming "Nature" as the model upon which to base standards of human behavior. She ridicules ideas of differential intelligence that claim inherent superiority for the male "sect." Knowing that the language itself limits or expands the parameters of meaning, she honors "foremothers" and questions the intended universality of the word *he*. In fact, except for matters of overt sexuality, there is little that Holley overlooks as her Samantha engages the contradictions, paradoxes, and inconsistencies that lie barely beneath the surface of ideas and values that deprive women of equality.

In the process, Holley does not ignore women's frailties. Women can be "meaner than pusley" about some things. Samantha always goes to a quilting early because you "can't be backbited to your face." Quiltings "jest sets women to slanderin' as easy and beautiful as any thing you ever see" (70). Like Frances Whitcher before her, Holley decries vicious gossip among women. (Though Samantha likewise points out the tendency for men to gossip as well.) Furthermore, contrary to Betsey's claim that women wouldn't have time to cast their ballots, Samantha counters: "Wimmen find time for thier everlastin' tattin' and croshain'. They find plenty of time for thier mats, and their tidys, their flirtations, thier feather flowers, and bead flowers, and hair flowers, and burr flowers, and oriental paintins, and Grecian paintins, and face paintins. They spend more time a frizzin' thier front hair than they would, to learn the whole constitution by heart . . . but when it comes to an act as simple and short as puttin' a letter into the post office, they are dreadful short on it for time" (228).

And again taking on sentimental fiction as an unworthy diversion for women who could undertake more significant study:

> . . . s'posin these soft, fashionable wimmen should read a little about the nation she lives in, and the laws that protects her if she keeps 'em, and hangs and imprisons her if she breaks 'em? I don't know but it would be as good for her, as to pore over novels all day long. . . these very wimmen that think the President's bureau is a chest of draws where he keeps his fine shirts, and the tariff is a wild horse the senators keep to ride out on,—these very wimmen that can't find time to read the constitution, let 'em get on to the track of a love-sick hero and a swoonin' heroine, and they will wade through half a dozen volumes. . . . Says I, in a deep camp meetin' voice, "if there had been a woman hid on the Island of Patmos, and Paul's letters to the churches had been love letters to her, there wouldn't be such a thick coat of dust on bibles as there is now." (228–29)

Despite her disagreements with Betsey on ideology and her distaste for sentimentality, Samantha nevertheless expresses solidarity with women. Neither Josiah nor anyone else should make fun of Betsey to please her. "I always make it a rule to stand up for my own sect."

And to reinforce the idea that all women don't think one way and all men another, she describes men who believe in equal rights in glowing terms as follows:

> I can tell a man that is for wimmin's rights as fur as I can see 'em. There is a free, easy swing to thier walk—a noble look to thier faces—thier big hearts and soles love liberty and justice, and bein' free themselves they want everybody else to be free. These men haint jealous of a woman's influence—haint afraid that she won't pay him proper respect if she haint obleeged to—and they needn't be afraid, for these are the very men that wimmin look up to, and worship,—and always will. A good, noble, true man is the best job old natur ever turned off her hands, or ever will—a man, that would wipe off a baby's tears as soft as a woman could, or "die with his face to the foe." (85–86)

As illustrated earlier, Samantha tackles the notion of separate spheres that serves to deny women the right to participate in public affairs. She not only points out the inconsistencies between genteel ideas and common sense, but she also exposes contradictions within the genteel value system itself. For example, dancing with a stranger is apparently acceptable but walking to the polling place is not. This exchange with Betsey explores the curious definitions of "public" and "private":

> "Betsey, is it any worse for a female woman to dress herself in a modest and Christian manner, with a braige viel over her face, and a brass mounted parasol in her hand, and walk decently to the pole and lay her vote on it, than to be introduced to a man, who for all you know may be a retired pirate, and have him walk up and hug you by the hour, to the music of a fiddle and a base violin?
>
> "But if you vote you have got to go before a board of men, and how tryin' to delicacy that would be.
>
> "I went before a board of men when I joined the meetin' house, and when I got the premium for my rag carpet, and I still live and call myself a respectable character, but," says I in a vein of unconcealed sarcasm "if these delicate ball characters are too modest to go in broad daylight armed with a umbrell before a venerable man settin' on a board, let 'em have a good old female board to take thier votes...." (225)

Samantha goes on to enumerate the variety of boards currently served on by women: boards at charity schools, fairs, hospitals, "penitentarys," picnics, and African missions. Casting and receiving votes would be no more public business, she claims, than "to sell Episcopal pin cushiens, Methodist I scream, or Baptist water melons, by the hour to a permiscuus crowd." (226)

Priding herself on her "megum" approach to life, Samantha "walks all the way around a topic before makin' pronouncements about it." When it comes to fashion, she walks around in a sensible "alapaca" with an overskirt, looking askance at both the trousers worn by Civil War surgeon Dr. Mary Walker and the bustles and corsets donned by "fashionable women." In her description of a women's rights lecturer, she applies her moderate approach to both the lecturer's ideas and her mode of dress. And the woman is found lacking on both counts. Claiming that women's rights lecturers generally call forth admiration and enthusiasm from her very "boozum," Samantha takes exception to the "wild-eyed ones that don't use no reason." These women constantly refer to "tyrant man" and not only want women to secure their rights but want men to lose theirs along the way. The reader knows that Samantha will not approve of this woman's ideas because she is introduced via a description of her appearance—an appearance reflecting the falseness, excess, and danger of current standards of fashionable dress. "Of all the painted, and frizzled, and ruffled, and humped up, and laced down critters I ever see, she was the cap sheaf. She had a hump [bustle] on her back bigger than any camel's I ever see to a managery, and no three wimmen ever grew the hair that critter had piled on to her head" (337).

As the woman continues to preach about "tyrant man," Samantha remembers that Josiah is a man, after all, and is steeled by principle to give the lecturer a piece of her mind:

"No wonder men don't think that we know enough to vote when they see the way some wimmen rig themselves out. Why" says I, "a bachelder that had always kept house in a cave, that had read about both but hadn't never seen neither, would as soon take you for a dromedary as a woman. . . . Much as I respect and honor Horace Greeley, if that pureminded and noble man should rig himself out with a bustle and trailin' pantaloons, I wouldn't vote for him, and Josiah shouldn't neither."

But she went right on without mindin' me—"Man has always tried to dwarf our intellects; cramp our souls. The sore female heart pants for freedom. It is sore! and it pants."

> Her eyes was rolled up in her head, and she had lifted both hands in a eloquent way, as she said this, and I had a fair view of her waist, it wasn't much bigger than a pipe's tail. And I says to her in a low, friendly tone. "Seein' we are only females present, let me ask you in a almost motherly way, when your heart felt sore and pantin' did you ever loosen your cosset strings? Why," says I, "no wonder your heart feels sore, no wonder it pants, the only wonder is, that it don't get discouraged and stop beatin' at all." (342–43)

Samantha disparages her dress and disagrees with her premise, but she affirms the lecturer's commitment to the vote, not because men are the "worst critters in the world," but because she wants justice done to every human being. "Justice never hurt nobody yet, and rights given through courtesy and kindness, haint so good in the long run, as rights given by law" (343)."Justice to wimmen won't prevent charitable men from bein' charitable, generous men from bein' generous, and good men from bein' good, while it will restrain selfishness and tyrany. One class was never at the mercy of another, in any respect, without that power bein' abused in some instances. Wimmen havin' the right to vote haint a goin' to turn the world over to once, and make black, white, in a minute, not by no means. But I sincerely believe it will bring a greater good to the female race and to the world" (344).

When Samantha walks around the topic of "free love," she is unequivocal in condemning it and "nerved by principle" to enlighten any misguided proponents. To show that sentimentality is not an exclusively female trait, Holley offers two male poet-orators. Professor Aspin Todd, Esq., writes airy poetry full of long words and sorrowful phantoms haunting the soul. Professor Theron Gusher is a "soarin' sole" who lectures in support of free love; he wants everyone to find "their affinitee." Samantha lectures him, suggesting a change of venue in his preoccupation: "Hain't there no cornfields where you could hire out for a scare-crow—can't you get to be a United States Senator? Hain't there no other mean job not quite so mean as this, you could get into?" (200).

In a scene that features many people at the forefront of the women's rights movement, Samantha visits the home of Victoria Woodhull. Also visiting are Dr. Mary Walker, Isabella Beecher Hooker, Susan B. Anthony, and Elizabeth Cady Stanton—all of whom Samantha admires. Before she gains entrance in her mission to scold "Victory" about her position on free love, Samantha encounters a man who divorced after dinner yesterday and married again before daylight, and mistakes

Samantha for his new wife, whose countenance and name are a mystery to him.

Thus satirizing the extremes of the transient, superficial nature of "affinitees," Samantha begins her talk with Victory and Theodore Tilton by acknowledging that Woodhull is both "in the right on it" and "in the wrong on it." Samantha admires Woodhull's stand on children's rights, health, and women's voting. But Victory is wrong in advocating divorce and free love. As Samantha marshals her arguments to set Woodhull straight, Victory counters with examples of wife abuse that surely justify gaining one's freedom. She requires no ceremony to tie her to her husband, she says, only the sacred tie of love.

Samantha calls on her experience with Josiah and on the Gospel in her affirmation of sticking to one's lawful mate. Holley establishes distance between herself and her literary persona when she allows Samantha to think she has made convincing arguments that in the end surely will persuade Woodhull. However, the reader knows that Woodhull's arguments are likewise persuasive and that she remains unconvinced and unconverted by Samantha's eloquence.

Just as she holds strong opinions about fashion and free love, Samantha abhors a double standard. Women have no inherent claim to goodness. And a double standard of conduct should not be invoked to justify errant behavior. Or, as Samantha says it, "I don't see why there shouldn't be he angels, as well as she ones." Actions that are coarse and shameful in women are likewise contemptible in men. She is proud that she has reared a son to believe that what is wrong for his sister is equally wrong for him. Samantha wonders why so many mothers will worry themselves to death about their daughters getting into bad company and bringing disgrace onto the family but do not fret about their sons. Not surprisingly, Josiah had not agreed with this approach to child rearing, believing a boy would cut up and act out occasionally. So it might have been acceptable to him for Thomas Jefferson to go to the circus and smoke tobacco and drink spirits—all of which were activities frowned upon by the Methodist Church—because "it don't look so bad for a boy as it does for a girl." But in a tactic this good Methodist would not have carried out but used as effective illustration, Samantha had early on won the day by threatening to send Tirzah Ann to the circus, buy her a pipe, and let her hang around barrooms if her brother had so ventured.

In her visit with Horace Greeley during his campaign against Ulysses S. Grant, Samantha marshals her strongest arguments, most homey metaphors, and eminent good sense in her effort to persuade a noble presidential candidate to "examine your platform, and see if there hain't no loose boards in it where some of the citizens of the United States, such as wimmen can fall through" (373).

In this chapter, Holley consolidates the political, economic, social, religious, and biological arguments proffered to deny women their rights and counters them in an arena where Samantha's "eppisodin'" could in fact affect government policy if Greeley were to accept her counsel and prevail in the election. When Horace protests that he can't imagine what rights women would want beyond what they have now, Samantha "dove right into the subject that was nearest to my heart (with the exception of Josiah)": "Horace, we want the right of equal pay for equal laber. The right of not bein' taxed without representation. The right of not bein' compelled, if she is a rich woman, of lettin' her property go to support public men, who are makin' laws that are ruinin' them she loves best, such as givin' licences to ruin body and soul. The right to stand by the side of all good and true soles in the nation, and tryin' to stop this evil spirit of intemperance and licentiousness that is runnin' rampant through the land" (374).

Horace offers the horror of indelicacy, a fate worse than death, if women "mingle in the wild vortex of political life." Women should influence indirectly through their husbands and sons. Samantha points out that all women don't have children to "mould" and that women should not "go to mouldin' men on the sly." Women influence politics in Washington as it is, through the offices of "female lobsteresses." She thinks good women should have as much influence as bad ones in political affairs.

Horace argues that women's minds are too weak to grasp public matters, "they are not logical, they have not the firm grasp of mind, the clear comprehension requisite to a voter" (379). Holley here embraces the nativist strain of the suffrage movement when she resorts to the negative ethnic stereotype of the ignorant, drunken Irishman. She claims that men in general would no doubt get ahead of women in selling their votes or voting the most times in one day—after all, they've had so much more practice. And she asks Horace to choose the better voter:

> . . . Elizabeth Cady Stanton gettin' up off of her religious knees in the mornin' after family prayers, and walkin'—with the Constitution in one hand and the Bible in the other—cooly and sensibly to the pole, or Patrick oh Flanegan comin' out of a drunken wake, and staggerin' up against the pole with a whisky bottle in one hand and a club in the other,

when he didn't know nothin' in the first place, and then had lost half or 3 quarters of that, in the liquer some clear minded, logical man give him, for votin' a few dozen times for him? (379)

Even her apt arguments become a failure of her "sect" when Horace acknowledges her powers of persuasion and deems them inappropriate. "You put the case in a very strong light Josiah Allen's wife. That is one of the peculiar weaknesses of your sect. You dont possess sufficient moderation. You exaggerate too much" (380). Like Josiah and so many others who would deny women their rights, Horace returns to the separate sphere argument and remains convinced that public duties would transform women into coarse, unfeminine creatures who would lose love for home and family. Even more absurdly, there might be "a lady blacksmith! a lady constable! a lady president!"

Samantha posits that a lady president is no more absurd than a lady queen and conjures the image of Queen Victoria. A close look at the "Widder Albert," she says, finds a loving mother of a houseful of children and devoted wife whose public duties were considerably more wearing than the annual exercise of the franchise. And her heart almost broke when Albert died.

Society has offered a false dichotomy between public and private spheres, Samantha argues, for one invariably informs the other. They are not opposites, forever exclusionary, where one is either dragged down into political affairs or raised up by the bonds of domestic happiness.

> The idee of its hurtin' a woman to know a little somethin', is in my mind awful simple. That was what the slaveholders said about the black Africans—it would hurt 'em to know too much. That is what Mr. Pope says to day about his church members. But I say that any belief, or custom that relies on oppression and ignorance and weakness to help it on in any degree, ought to be exploded up. Beautiful weakness and simplicity, haint my style at all in the line of women. I have seen beautiful simplicities before now, and they are always affected, selfish critters, sly, underhanded, their minds all took up with little petty gossip and plottin's. Why they can't set a teacup on the table in a open-hearted noble way. They have to plot on some byway to get it there, unbeknown to somebody. Their mouths have been drawed so into simpers, that they couldn't laugh a open generous laugh to save their lives. Always havin' some spear ready under their soft mantilly, to sweetly spear some other woman in the back. Horace, they haint my style. Beautiful weakness and simplicity may do for one evenin' in a ball room. But it don't wear well

for all the cares and emergencies that come in a life of from 40 to 50 years. (382–83)

Horace finally resorts to the fail-safe argument of Nature. Nature meant for the male of every species to be preeminent. Even the wisest of men may err when they make their laws, but Nature is unerring. Nature never makes mistakes. Samantha eagerly calls this view into question by turning to Nature "herself" for examples. Nature is indeed unerring and Nature has made queen bees. "Old Nature herself clapped the crown on to 'em. You never heard of king bees, did you?" And you won't find any more industrious, "equinomical," orderly doin's in any nation than she has in "hern." The bees work "stiddy" as can be in the morning and are back safely in the hive at night. There's no speculatin' on other people's honey encouraged. Samantha does acknowledge one problem with the arrangements, and is quick to say that she doesn't approve of it. If the male bees can't make enough honey to last the entire hive throughout the entire winter, well, they kill off the male bees. She thinks they hadn't "ort" to kill off all those lazy drone husband bees just to keep from winterin' 'em, but then every law of Nature has its little eccentricities and this is "hern." Outside of that, though, many men in high chairs should look to the Queen Bee as a pattern of the "Executive Female."[2]

Sidestepping Samantha's logic on Nature, Horace takes refuge in the Creator, who he says fashioned women for a quiet, home life. "God never designed her to go rantin' round in public, preachin' and lecturin" (386). Holley then takes on the secular issue of the propriety of women speaking in public, and even further, the sacred matter of women being preachers. In the process, this religious woman, who often started her morning by pointing to a verse in the Bible that would be her guide for the day, suggests a reading of the Good Book that places it in a historic context of time, place, and culture.

Samantha disavows a need to speak publicly herself, but she affirms those who receive the call, male or female. She reasons that God purposely made the grasshoppers "loose jinted" so they could jump and the birds full throated so they could sing. If He hadn't meant for them to do it, "He wouldn't have put it into 'em." Just so with humans: "And when the Lord has put eloquence, and inspiration, and enthusiasm into a human sole, you can't help it from breakin' out. I say it is right for a woman to talk, if she has got anything to say for God and humanity. I have heard men and wimmen both, talk when they hadn't nothin' to say,

and it is jest as tiresome in a man, as it is in a woman, in my opinion
... (387–88).

When Horace objects by invoking Paul's declaration that it was a shame for women to speak in public, in one reply Samantha brings "Mr. Paul" down to the level of a mere man (and a "likely old bachelder" at that), tweaks the idea of inspiration as justification, argues for the primacy of the example of Jesus, and places scripture in its historic context:

> Men will quote Mr Paul's remarks concernin' wimmen not preachin', and say he was inspired when he said that, and I say to 'em, "how is it about folks not marryin', he speaks full as pinted about that?" "Oh!" they say, "he wazzn't inspired when he said that," and I say to 'em, "how can you tell—when a man is 18 or 19 hundred years older than you be—how can you tell when he was inspired and when he wazzn't, not bein' a neighbor of his'en." And after all, Mr. Paul didn't seem to be so awful set on this subject, for he went right on to tell how a woman's head ought to be fixed when she was a prayin' and a prophecyin'.
>
> But in my opinion, all that talk about wimmen was meant for that church he was a writin' to, for some reason confined to that time, and don't apply to this day, or this village—and so with marryin'. When a man was liable to have his head cut off any minute, or to be eat up by lions, it wazzn't convenient to marry and leave a widder and a few orphan's. That is my opinion, other folks have thiern. But let folks quarell all they have a mind to, as to whether Mr. Paul was inspired when he wrote these things, or whether he wazzn't, this *we know*, that Jesus is a divine pattern for us to follow, and He chose a woman to carry the glad tidin's of His resurrection to the brethren. There was one woman who received her commission to preach right from the Almighty. (388–89; emphasis in original)

But regardless of the specific subject of Samantha's reasonings, her listener—whether Horace or Josiah or Betsey, et al.—ignores the specific and returns again and again to the general old theme: wedlock is woman's true "spear." In Horace's case, Samantha must rescue him from the ardent Betsey who agrees totally with his views, inquires rather too cheerfully about the failing health of his wife, pleads for a strand of his hair, and generally makes herself available to take his wife's place when she has the decency to "drop off." It is the specter of Betsey's "too zealous carryin' out" of her spear that finally budges Horace from his stance and leaves him admitting that any "new state of public affairs that would make woman more independent of matrimony, less zealous, less reckless in handlein' that spear, might be more or less beneficial both to herself, and to man" (395).

Horace's "conversion" is occasioned not by the sound logic of Samantha but by the vision of his ideas incarnate in Betsey as she tries to cling to him. Nevertheless, having completed her lofty mission in the Cause of Right, Samantha can go home. At the end of *My Opinions*, after a perilous voyage by boat during a storm, she returns to home and Josiah, complete with scenes of endearing, if restrained, affection between the lawful "pardners."

In the extended allegory that is *My Opinions*, all the literary elements are set in place that will serve Holley's continuing agenda for social justice: the travel motif, the dialect humor, the tension between vernacular and genteel/rural and urban, the mockery of sentimentality, the use of domestic metaphor, the rich detail of daily life observed and described and validated, and the restoration of domestic tranquillity at book's end.

In "How I Wrote My First Books" Holley alludes with amusement to the notion that so many people assumed *My Opinions* had been written by a man. An elderly gentleman speaking to one of Holley's relatives declared his "high opinion of the man that wrote that book." When told it was written by a woman, he remained resolute and unshaken: "That book was written by a *man*." Holley's dry rejoinder: "I have always supposed it was a compliment" (404; emphasis in original).

Holley said that she put everything she knew into *My Opinions*.[3] It must, then, have presented a considerable challenge to write twenty additional books over the ensuing forty years. But of course there was more that she knew. And through Samantha she "put [her] shoulder blades to the wheel" and "eppisoded" for social justice into the second decade of the next century.

Chapter Three

Gentility and the Sentimental Tradition: *Samantha at Saratoga, or, Flirtin' with Fashion*

After *My Opinions and Betsey Bobbet's*, in 1877 Holley published the first of her travel books centering on an exposition, *Josiah Allen's Wife as a P. A. and P. I.: Samantha at the Centennial*. That was followed by two works in 1880, *The Lament of the Mormon Wife* and *My Wayward Pardner, or, My Trials with Josiah, America, the Widow Bump, and Etcetery*, written in response to what she saw as a particular social problem: polygamy. In 1883 Holley traded on the fame of Josiah Allen's Wife to publish *Miss Richards' Boy and Other Stories*, an unsuccessful volume that carried Holley's name as author and offered stories in "good English" that were not unlike the works of E. D. E. N. Southworth, Susan Warner, and other sentimental fiction writers of the day. Others capitalized on the popularity of Holley's dialect sketches by simply pirating them. So eager was J. S. Ogilvie of New York City to publish *Samantha at Saratoga* that when he was outbid by Hubbard of Philadelphia, he appropriated a chapter from *My Opinions* for the title story, used Holley's pseudonym as author, and issued *Miss Jones's Quilting and Other Stories* (1887).[1] Ogilvie's business instincts, if not his ethics, were on target, for the book he lost to Hubbard became Holley's best-selling novel, a comedy of manners that hoisted gentility on its own petard.

As mentioned in the previous chapter, Marietta Holley initially explored the relationship between sentimentality, genteel ideology, and the cause of women's rights in *My Opinions*. She ridiculed the conventions of sentimental and Gothic fiction in the preface and then created in Betsey the quintessential frail flower of sentimentality as foil. With her alliterative name, clinging vine inclinations, and irrepressible authorship of "dretful" poetry, Betsey Bobbet was a caricature through whom Holley satirized both the nineteenth-century sentimental female poet and her product.

Of course, Holley was not alone in eyeing that particular target. In "Wit, Sentimentality and the Image of Women in the Nineteenth Century," Nancy Walker contends that witty women writers of the nineteenth century—"Fanny Fern," Caroline Kirkland, Frances Whitcher, "Gail Hamilton," and Marietta Holley—"consistently satirized the woman who wrote pious, sentimental prose and poetry. Their efforts to demote this figure from the high status accorded her by genteel society were part of their rebellion against widely held notions of woman's 'proper' role in American culture."[2] To that end, Walker explains, the "popular image of the woman writer as soggy sentimentalist" was more than a stock comic character. "In the work of women humorists, it became the embodiment of all that these women knew themselves not to be: weak, dependent, illogical. . . . Almost every nineteenth-century female humorist felt the need to create and demolish this image as if exorcising a demon which would have prevented her from writing humor" (20).

Besides Betsey Bobbet, Holley's works are peopled with an assortment of other characters who talk and/or act like protagonists in a sentimental novel. For example, the Widder Doodle accepted Solomon Cypher's marriage proposal (just three weeks after his wife's death) because he "offered himself in a dretful handsome style . . . she said the childern of the Abbey, or Thadeus of Warsaw couldn't done it up in any more foamin' and romantic way. . . ."[3] That proposal would no doubt make up for his haste to take her home to replace the hired girl, his domineering attitude, and his inability to be a good provider. In *Samantha Among the Brethren*, the unmarried Serena Fogg had presented a lecture called "Wedlock's Peaceful Repose" in "pretty talk" filled with analogies about married life.[4] Samantha faults her for not being at all "megum." After three years of marriage to a butcher (which has been blessed with two pairs of twins), Serena writes to Samantha acknowledging Samantha's wisdom in the matter. Samantha muses: "Wall, she has wrote dretful flowery on wedlock, and its perfect, unbroken calm, and peaceful repose, and now she has had a realizin' sense of what it really is" (26). Of course, the irony is that Holley's sense of what marriage was like was observed secondhand.[5] Nevertheless, the unmarried Holley wrote 20 books in which married life was the cornerstone from which to argue an agenda that, if enacted, would alter the traditional norms of that very institution.

The sentimental tradition in nineteenth-century prose featured characters exhibiting excesses of emotionalism, frailty, "consummate uselessness,"[6] pious religiosity, vanity, false pride, passivity, and general foolishness. Poems featured contrived rhymes, awkward grammar, and flowery language. These attributes served to endorse the genteel code, a middle-class and upper-middle-class phenomenon dating from the 1830s, whose assumptions and restrictions were attacked by women humorous writers. In *Women's Humor in the Age of Gentility*, Linda Morris catalogs the targets: "Women's idleness, their presumed helplessness, their growing obsession with material goods and social status, their relegation to the private sphere, their economic dependence on men—all these tendencies became prime targets in women's humor from the 1830s to the 1870s, culminating in Marietta Holley's identification of gentility, per se, as the principal obstacle standing in women's way of achieving full political equality with men."[7]

In discussing the work of Ann Stephens, Frances Whitcher, and Holley, Morris rightly claims that both male and female vernacular humorists addressed the impact of genteel values on American society. But unlike their male counterparts, the women humorists "did not equate gentility with femininity; indeed, they understood that women were particularly oppressed by the genteel code."[8]

Holley suggests that subscribing to the affectations of gentility is not merely foolish; it is dangerous. In addition to Samantha's previously discussed admonitions about "beautiful weakness and simplicity" to Betsey, Josiah, and Horace Greeley in *My Opinions*, Holley revisits the theme regularly and mounts a concentrated attack on the ideals and values of genteel society in *Samantha at Saratoga* (1887). In *My Wayward Pardner* (1880) Holley brings the issue into Samantha's home, not only in the person of Josiah who is, of course, hopeless, but also embodied in daughter Tirzah Ann, whose only major weakness is her sentimentality. Tirzah Ann is determined to keep up with Miss Skidmore who sits in "stunny, motionless autitudes and postures" claiming that "nobody who made any pretensions to bein' genteel stayed to home durin' the heated term" (287). The practical Samantha naturally disagrees, figuring that Tirzah Ann, her husband Whitfield, and baby are healthy, rested, and happy at home and should leave well enough alone. In noting Miss Skidmore's haughty demeanor, Samantha suggests that "camfrey roots" and burdock leaves would limber up that stiff neck. But hers was a condition cured only by common sense and a true dignity; burdock couldn't help. Despite Samantha's counsel, her daughter's healthy family goes away "on a exertion after rest and pleasure" and returns much the worse for wear—Tirzah Ann on a bed, Whitfield with two canes and his arm in a sling, and the baby feeble and pale.

In *Samantha Among the Brethren* a poor but sensible man had worked hard to put back money to buy a house and security for his wife and family. But when he died, his wife (she of the "showy education, showy weddin', and showy' settin'-out") and her parents were so concerned with appearances that they spent all the money on fancy mourning clothes, funeral, reception, and monument. Bankrupt, the wife/mother soon dies and the children are carted off to the poorhouse, innocent victims of a misguided need to follow genteel form. As Samantha said of the parents' "showy-lookin'" house, "more pains had been took with the porticos and ornaments than with the underpinnin'" (128).

The theme continues into the twentieth century in *Samantha vs. Josiah* with Josiah's relationship to an automobile he borrows for a month. To be properly stylish, he wears strange outfits and pretends to be working on the car. He even thinks it is preferable to scare horses and muddy people rather than be a courteous driver because it is so genteel and stylish to cause a ruckus with one's "orto." Finally he has a wreck and is bedridden with his injuries.[9] Furthermore, Josiah perceives what we would call white-collar crime as simply another exercise in stylishness. Always scheming to make a lot of money, he decides to fake his death and collect the insurance money. After all, other people steal hand over fist, in a nice way, and then go abroad. To Samantha's moral protestations, he replies: ". . . you're never willin' for me to be stylish and fashinable and make money as other smart genteel men do" (268). Again, the consequences of aspirations to gentility exceed appearances of foolhardiness.

Though both men and women are subject to contamination by the infection of gentility spreading across the country, the identification of these values with women's proper sphere is the most pernicious side effect. In *Samantha at the Centennial* (1877) Holley lambasts the hypocrisy of genteel manners and ridicules insincere and misplaced emotionalism when Samantha visits the Spicer family. Mahala has married a man of comfortable means but spends every minute cleaning. So obsessed is she with how the big house will look, she shuts it up and lives in the wood-house, laboring over endless ruffles in which to clothe restricted children who must not get dirty. Delila Ann, on the other hand, has married a poor man who needs her help. But in the interests of gentility, she does not allow their seven daughters to do anything but dress up to "catch a bo," attend to visiting rituals, read dime novels, and dote on dogs. Her husband is so strapped trying to pay the milliner's bills that he can't even afford a Bible. When she discovers that the effusive sobbing and sighing in this self-proclaimed house of mourning is directed at the demise of a dog, Samantha proclaims it a House of Sham. She offers unsolicited advice: "Is marryin' the only theme that anybody can lay holt of? . . . Nobody but a fool would lay holt of a hook baited with dime novels, lazyness, deceitfulness, and pups. Learn your girls to be industrious and to respect themselves. . . . No woman can feel honorable and reverential towards themselves, when they are a foldin' their useless hands over their empty souls, waitin' for some man—no matter who—to marry 'em and support 'em (312).

In fact, Samantha feels so strongly about the transgressions of gentility that she connects them with the sin of adultery. "There is two words in the English language that I feel cold, and almost hauty towards, and they are 'affinity,' such as married folks hunt after, and 'genteel.' I wish," says I, "that these two words would join hands and elope the country; I'd love to see their backs, as they sot out, and bid 'em a glad farewell" (308).

As Holley's own mode of dress illustrated, she did not see good taste in women's fashions, as reflected in the wearing of silks and brocades, to be incompatible with the cause of women's rights. But through Samantha she castigates fashionable excesses. And though Holley was herself a rural woman whose appearance more nearly resembled a "Grand Duchess" than her homely character,[10] she nevertheless satirized the tendency of country folk to imitate genteel, urban sophisticates. Women, in particular, Samantha argues, have given in to the tyranny of fashion, dictated by "old They."

> *They*, . . . who is old *They* that is leadin' my sect into chains and slavery? . . . Bring him up to me, and lemme wrastle with him, and destroy him. . . . If he gives the word, wimmen will drop their dresses right down a yard into the mud, or tack 'em up to their knees; they will puff 'em out like baloons, or pin 'em back, a bandegin' themselves like mummies; they will wear their bunnets on the back of their necks leavin' their faces all out in the sun, or they will wear 'em over their forwards, makin' 'em as blind as a bat. . . . Fashion is king and *They* is his prime minister and factorum; and between 'em both, wimmen is bound hand and foot, body and soul. And . . . would that some female Patrick Henry or George Washington would rise up and set 'em free from them tyrants. (*Centennial*, 287–88)

All of these strains—the image of the sentimental female poet, the foolishness and danger of genteel pretensions, the tyranny of fashion—converge in what eventually became Holley's best-selling book.[11]

Samantha at Saratoga

Samantha at Saratoga, or, Flirtin' with Fashion was first published in 1887 and became that year's best-seller.[12] It was unusual among the books using a travel motif in that Holley actually visited Saratoga Springs, New York, before she wrote about it. In fact, she and her fellow discoverer, Mrs. Sophie Smith, were such zealous seekers of "all the highways and byways," the "odd and picturesque" of Saratoga Springs that they were called "The Tramps" by their friends. She penned the manuscript in a quiet room at the top of a large boardinghouse during "the whole of one golden summer" in Saratoga Springs and sold it for $10,000. Holley clearly enjoyed being both participant and observer during the high season at the most fashionable racing resort of the day in upstate New York.[13]

In some ways this book most thoroughly devoted to the enactors of the genteel tradition is the least pointed of Holley's works about specific women's rights issues. In the preface to *Samantha at Saratoga,* Samantha imagines the lives of the Old Testament prophets as she compares the tradition of just staying home to the yearly exodus to "spahs" in order to rest. She surmises that our "4 fathers" must have gotten "real rested," sitting as they did for several hundred years in one spot. Miss Abraham and Miss Isaac were no doubt "stay to home women." And when they did move, it was pretty simple: just "hist" up the tent and throw it across a camel's back. Samantha lists all the preparations one must make to fill those 8 or 10 Saratoga trunks with gowns for every conceivable occasion and decides that old Miss Abraham would be so tuckered that she'd be a dead "4 mother." If, that is, she weren't already.

Civilization has advantages, she muses, but some of the simple joys are being lost. "Yes, the hull nation is in a hurry to get somewhere else, to go on, it can't wait" (17). Holley uses the context of Saratoga Springs's reputation as a watering spa to expose the false values of form over content and again affirm rural, common-sense values. Samantha observes the form—parades and parasols, piazzas and poetry, fashions and flirting, curative waters, "civilized agonies," and genteel diversions—and finds them decidedly deficient in the cardinal virtue of "megumness."

Ironically, it is Samantha who first suggests a trip to Saratoga ("mebbe it will help Josiah's corns"). Initially reluctant, Josiah then plunges into the fashionableness of it all with abandon, trimming off his "honorable side whiskers" and cultivating a "little patch on the end of his chin."

Gentility and the Sentimental Tradition

Though counseled by the sisters of the church on the kind of low-necked, corseted fashion expected of her at a "spah," Samantha determines to travel there as an example of sensible modesty and good health.

> ... as fer the waists bein' all girted up and drawed in, that is nothin' but crushed bones and flesh and vitals, that is just crowdin' down your insides into a state o' disease and deformity, torturin' your heart down so's the blood can't circulate, and your lungs so's you can't breathe, it is nothin' but slow murder anyway, and if I ever take it into my head to kill myself. ... I haint a goin' to do it in a way of perfect torture and torment to me, I'd ruther be drownded.
> ... I am one that is goin' to take good long breaths to the very last. (38–39)

She wears a high-necked black "alpacky" and assumes that when women see her they will "pause in their wild career, and cover up their necks and pull their sleeves down" (157). On that score, she is, of course, disappointed.

In the figure of wealthy Miss George Washington Flamm, Holley lampoons a genteel devotion to dogs at the expense of all else, as she had in *Samantha at the Centennial*, and underscores the foolishness of suggestions to make statues more fashionable, as she would do again in *Samantha at the World's Fair* (1893). In Miss Flamm she concentrates the "sins" of the fashionable life lived for its own sake and moralizes about the empty successes and far-ranging consequences of such vacuous pursuit. Miss Flamm lavishes constant affection on her dog but can't care for her children. They are being brought up by nurses, Miss Flamm being so very *delicate* in health. That delicacy can be traced to her disfiguring mode of dress. The sleeves on her dresses are so tight that her hands look "kinder bloated and swelled all the time." And she can't breathe better because her waist is so "drawed in" that "it wuzn't much bigger than a pipe's tail." Furthermore, "she can't get her hands to her head to save her, and if a assassin should strike her, she couldn't raise her arm to ward off the blow if he killed her. I s'pose it worrys her" (296).

Miss Flamm is willing to do anything *necessary* for a waist that tapers. In fact, the only fault she finds with the "Godduss of Liberty" enlightening the world in New York "Harber" is the way she looks.

> If that Goddus only had corsets on, and sleeves that wuz skin tight, and her overskirt looped back over a bustle, it would be perfect!"

But I [Samantha] told her I liked her looks as well ag'in as she wuz. Why, sez I, "How could she lift her torch above her head? And how could she ever enlighten the world, if she wuz so held down by her corsets and sleeves that she couldn't wave her torch?" (296–97)[14]

Attention only to outward appearance, then, can endanger even liberty itself, especially justice and equality for women. Indeed, it is not only one's own health and safety that is imperiled by the forms of gentility. Miss Flamm is so wrapped up in her dog that she neglects to supervise her children's nurse. As a result, her young daughter nearly dies from an "axident." Only when her daughter lies near death does Miss Flamm finally discard the dog, discover her motherhood, and reorder her priorities.[15]

Of course, no "spah" would be complete without the healing waters and the sentimental poet. Josiah, he of the careful economy, drinks lavishly of the noble water (all you can drink for five cents) because he is bound to get his money's worth. As he goes from Everlastin' Spring to Immortal Spring to Live-forever Spring, he drinks "more than wuz for his own good," and Samantha fears he has "drounded out" his insides. Because he is never "megum," he also pursues too diligently diversions such as tobogganing and flirting. Samantha describes his technique in the latter enterprise: "like an effort of our old mair to play a tune on the melodian, no grace in it . . ." (239).

Accompanying them from Jonesville to visit her relatives in Saratoga is Ardelia Tutt, whose mother brags that she can write poetry by the bagful on any topic—spring, a bench, trout, the roller coaster, whatever. Her exceptional talent as a poet is her *speed*. "Ardelia dashes off things with a speed that would astonish a mere common writer. Why she dashed off thirty-nine verses once while she was waitin' for the dish water to bile, and sent 'em right off to the printer, without glancin' at 'em agin" (58–59). She measures the lines with a stick to make sure they are the right length.[16] Though she is adored by her hometown baker, he is not "romanticule" enough and doesn't fit her image of a "genteel lover," and so she is temporarily infatuated with a less worthy rival in Saratoga who says he's a banker. Of course, it turns out the bank that was doing such heavy business was a sand bank, the deposits and withdrawals made in wheelbarrows.

By narrative's end, at least two of the worshipers of fashion and sentimentalism have learned a lesson. Miss Flamm is becoming a devoted mother. Ardelia marries the baker. Having thoroughly explored Saratoga and witnessed the rigors and results of a fashionable season, Samantha and Josiah return to Jonesville for the customary welcome back into the bosom of home, surrounded by those they love. Gentility has been condemned. Domesticity and common sense are once again affirmed and celebrated.

Chapter Four

Upholding Duty's Apron Strings: Temperance, Race, and Religion

In her role of humorist as truth teller, Holley engaged major social issues and institutions in an effort to unmask injustice and effect change. Her books depict Samantha as an unwavering proponent of prohibition, an opponent of racism who herself used racial stereotypes, and an admonishing believer dismayed by the workings of the institutional church.

Smashin' the Whisky Ring: Temperance

When Holley turned to the issue of temperance, as she often did, she reflected the ideas and tactics of the largest women's organization in the country, the Women's Christian Temperance Union (WCTU). Fueled by the enthusiasm of evangelical religion, the WCTU was initially a praying society of Midwestern women whose fervor erupted during the winter of 1873–74 when more than 60,000 women took to the streets to close local saloons, mainly in rural areas. Antebellum women reformers active first in the abolition movement and then the women's rights movement had been concerned with the temperance issue both as an abstract ideal and "because the law placed married women so much at the mercy of their husbands."[1] The post–Civil War activism picked up that temperance thread and launched what was to become an international quest. The saloon-closing crusade itself "lacked the structure capable of sustaining a lasting movement," but it "created a cohort of women permanently changed by their new experience of power."[2]

These were, by and large, conservative women of the churches who had not been receptive to the issues of greater rights for women. Frances Willard, who led the WCTU from 1879–99, saw the possibility of "harnassing women's newly released energies in a multipurpose organization which might work, not for temperance alone, but for a broad welfare program appealing to women, including woman suffrage both as means and end."[3] Of this new coalition Willard wrote: "They had never even seen a 'woman's rights convention,' and had been held aloof from the 'suffragists' by fears as to their orthodoxy; but now there were women prominent in all Church cares and duties eager to clasp hands for a more aggressive work than such women had ever before dreamed of undertaking."[4]

Willard used domestic imagery and the notion of gender spheres to justify the linking of temperance to broader social reform. She advocated reform in the name of purity and the home. Politics was "enlarged housekeeping." The goal was "Home Protection." Women could not protect their homes and families from liquor or other vices unless they had a voice in public affairs. That voice remained mute unless women could exercise the franchise, at least in local option ballots regarding the sale of intoxicants. Willard advanced, and the WCTU endorsed, a motto that drew in an ever-expanding cross section of women: "Do Everything." To that end, departments were created for channeling women's reform energies, among them: work in kindergartens, prisons, medical dispensaries and shelters; departments concerned with physical culture and hygiene, prostitution and mothers; and a department to work for the franchise.

Temperance and suffrage became linked in the public mind and that identification was perceived by many to hurt the suffrage cause. Frances Willard knew Holley's Samantha books and their power to persuade on both issues. She sent Holley temperance materials, invited her to appear at national conventions, and corresponded regularly. In "The Story of My Life" Holley quotes from a letter she received from Willard: "'Brave, sweet spirit; You don't know how much we all love you, no woman has more grandly helped the woman's cause.' And she wrote me in a letter from Evanston after reading my temperance book, 'Sweet Cicely': 'It doeth me good like medicine, a thousand blessings on you. You were inspired when you wrote that.'"[5]

In addition to materials received from Willard, Senator Henry Blair, and other sources, Holley cited firsthand knowledge of intemperance, as witnessed in an uncle by marriage, whose bright red face was "the bloody badge John Barleycorn bestows upon his victims in return for the ruin of their soul and body."[6] Likewise, True Williams, illustrator of many of her books as well as those of Mark Twain, "was an excellent artist when his enemy, John Barleycorn, was absent."[7] Holley proudly referred to temperance and woman suffrage as "the themes of many of my preachments, poured out with a constancy and zeal that would do credit to the most earnest reformer."[8]

And so Samantha's sermons on the evils of the Whiskey Trade and the license bill surface in several books as she "soars into eloquence" from her homely pulpit. In *My Opinions* she tackles the double standard as well as intemperate habits: "'Josiah Allen if Thomas Jefferson goes with those boys, and gets to chewin' and smokin' tobacco, I shall buy Tirzah Ann a pipe. [8] And about drinkin',' says I, 'Thomas Jefferson, if it should ever be the will of Providence to change you into a wild bear, I will chain you up and do the best I can by you. But if you ever do it yourself, turn yourself into a wild beast by drinkin', I will run away, for I never could stand it, never. And,' I continued, 'if I ever see you hangin' round bar-rooms and tavern doors, Tirzah Ann shall hang too'" (115). Liquor makes a fool and brute of anybody, she says, without stopping to ask about their "sect."

Some cautionary tale appears in nearly every book—a family brought to ruin by the father's drinking habits, the hypocrisy of exporting whiskey to China alongside religious tracts declaring that no drunkard can get into Heaven, the horror of a little girl's murder by an intoxicated man, the foolishness of Josiah's attempt to make the liquor trade genteel.[9] But it is in *Sweet Cicely* (1885) that Holley engages temperance as the main theme and inextricably connects it with the need for suffrage and the ruin brought to lives by women's powerlessness before the law.

A summary of the "plot" reads like many maudlin melodramas of the period. Cicely, whose smooth, white complexion looked a good deal like "the pure white leaves of the posy Sweet Cicely," is Josiah's niece. Samantha and Josiah took her in for a year when her mother died and "wus dretful good to her." Cicely later met and married Paul Slide, who was handsome, rich, and well-mannered—except for his habit of drinking. Alarmed by his weak chin and bouts of drinking, Samantha pleads with Cicely not to marry him, afraid he will break her heart. Paul convinces Cicely that her influence will redeem him. All seems to be going well until Paul's college chum comes to their village and opens a drinking saloon and billiard room. Paul becomes his best customer, and he refuses all entreaties to deny Paul liquor, placing the responsibility at the feet of the government that gave him a license. Ruined and desolate, Paul murders the saloon keeper over a game of billiards and would have been hanged had he not died in prison the night before his sentence was to be carried out.

A brokenhearted Cicely pledges to do whatever she can to save her son from the temptations that destroyed his father and begins by laying the blame for her husband's demise on the laws of the land. She must talk with legislators and determines to go to Washington, D.C. When Josiah decides to run for Senator (his main motive being money),

Samantha feels she must go to Washington "as a forerunner" to check it out. Among the interludes along the way of this narrative are a visit from an accident-prone, office-seeking relative, Josiah's experience with a free railroad pass, a wedding for their hired man, an episode with a sewing-machine salesman, and the like. When Samantha and Cicely finally make it to Washington, they are frustrated by the official logic that awaits them. In the end, Cicely dies with the hope that God will take care of her boy. "The grave was about the only place of safety that the Lord Himself could find for the boy," and so the last scene describes his death.

The Cicely story line is both serious and sentimental, with only an occasional "one-liner" to lighten the sense of helplessness and doom that attend her situation. It is mostly in the interchanges between Samantha and Josiah, or Samantha and the various politicians she encounters that Holley rescues the narrative from the manipulative morass of melodrama.

Samantha again takes on a range of issues, from women's trials with male drunkenness to the use of nature and the Bible to claim superiority for men, from the "sect" of public statues to the need for direct influence, from the need for protection against wife beating to advocacy of the female franchise.

In a nod to both genetic and environmental cause and effect, Samantha says Cicely's husband might have resisted temptation "if there hadn't been drinking-saloons right in front of that chin" (12). Holley comes close to current thinking on alcoholism as a disease, albeit through Samantha's worrying on Paul's facial features. People said that Paul could have stopped drinking if he had wanted to. Samantha disagrees: "Why anybody that had them [chin and lips] on 'em, and was made up inside and outside accordin', as folks be that have them looks; why, unless they was specially guarded by good influences, and fenced off from bad ones,—why, they *could not* exert any self-denial and control and firmness" (23; emphasis in original). Furthermore, Samantha follows "that chin and that mouth right back through seven generations of the Slide family" and makes a case for a family history of alcoholism. All of them who "had that face" got into trouble of some kind.

Women are powerless and vulnerable because the law, which claims to protect them from consorting in the unseemliness of the public sphere, in fact deprives them of control even of their own homes and moral consciences. Cicely brought her own property to her marriage, and legally that property became her husband's. When he died, he left a considerable estate to his son and a liberal yearly allowance to his wife. But it was the executor who managed the estate and the properties, and the executor invested money she had brought to the marriage in a manner that was anathema to her by renting space for saloons and gaming rooms. Because her property was the largest in the village, the taxes she paid "helped more than any thing else did to keep the streets smooth and even before the saloon-doors, so drunkards could get there easy" (69). The executor even uses her money to hire liquor votes. She can complain to him, plead with him, speak ill of him, but she has no legal recourse to compel him to act in accordance with her wishes and conscience. She leaves instructions that if both she and her son were to die, the estate was to be used to establish a home for children of drunkards. But while she lives, she is forced by the law of men to be an integral part of a contradiction—supporter of temperance and landlord of saloons. If she is to protect her young son and the children of other sad-eyed mothers from the evils of drink, she must have the ear of legislators and the clout of the ballot.

Josiah, who had voted for the license bill, of course claims that it would be unwomanly and perilous to "the domestic nature of wimmen" if they cast ballots. Voting is no more perilous to the domestic nature of women, says Samantha, than it was to take their hens to the fair. Despite the "turmoil of public life" at the fair, the hens made nests and hatched chickens. "I never heard a old hen called out of her spear, and unhenly, because she would fly out at a hawk, and cackle loud, and cluck, and try to lead her chickens off into safety. And while the rooster is a steppin' high, and struttin' round, and lookin' surprised and injured, it is the old hen that saves the chickens, nine times out of ten" (72). Cicely is trying to save her boy from the hawks, and lack of the franchise keeps her a slave to men of less education, "many of 'em who did not know a letter of the alphabet."

To Josiah's claim that the entire female "sect" would be lowered in the eyes of the entire male "sect" if they voted, Samantha replies: "They are ranked now by the laws of the United States, and the will of men, with idiots, lunatics, and criminals. . . . *There hain't any lower class that we can get into* than the ones we are in now" (76; emphasis in original).

When Josiah decides to run for political office, Samantha reminds him that he doesn't even know what "tariff and revenue" mean, and she makes him squirm about his intention to buy votes with apples, beer, rum, and whiskey. Via her trip to Washington, D.C., she determines to discourage him. When neighbors learn of her impending journey, they request that she do their "errents" while there. Through the "errents" of

Dorlesky Burpy and the catalog of misfortune that has befallen the Dorlesky Burpy family women, Samantha again applies mother-wit insight to reveal injustice embedded in the laws of the land.

Dorlesky Burpy comes for an all day visit and declares that Samantha is to tell the President that Dorlesky "wanted the Whiskey Ring destroyed, and she wanted her rights; and she wanted 'em both in less than 2 weeks." Dorlesky is a "vegetable widder" whose troubles—each and every one of them according to the law—had begun before she was born when her father willed her away to his brother. The law was on his side. Dorlesky's mother was powerless to protect her infant, torn away from her loving arms and delivered up to a "dissipated and mean" uncle. "It has always been the boast of our American law, that it takes care of wimmen. It took care of [Dorlesky's mother]. It held her in its strong, protectin' grasp, and held her so tight, that the only way she could slip out of it wus to drop into the grave, which she did in a few months. Then it leggo" (151).

But the law "kep' hold" of Dorlesky. The uncle bound her out in service to a woman who kept a "drinkin' den." Finally, helped by a good woman, she escaped, came to Jonesville to live, changed her name, and grew up "a nice, industrious girl." She inherited property from the woman at her death, married, and bore two children. But then her husband "took to drinkin'," neglected his business, and beat his wife. "He went accordin' to law; and the law of the United States don't approve of a man whippin' his wife enough to endanger her life—it says it don't. He made every move of hisen lawful, and felt that Dorlesky hadn't ort to complain and feel hurt. But a good whippin' will make anybody feel hurt, law or no law" (152).

Finally, she broke her hip falling on a sidewalk, her husband sued for $10,000, and of course claimed the money as his. While she was "layin' there achin' in splints," he took her "hip-money" to court another woman. "But the law gin it to him; and he was only availin' himself of the glorious liberty of our free republic, and doin' as he was a mind to" (153). Before she was out of the splints, he divorced her and "by the help of that money, and the Whiskey Ring, he got her two little children away from her" (154).

Several of the Burpy women have suffered because of the Whiskey Ring. Dorlesky's sister Susan Burpy Clapsaddle was in the poorhouse, though she had brought $5,000 of her own money to her marriage. Dorlesky accounts for where that property had gone: "It has gone down Philemon Clapsaddle's throat. Look down that man's throat, and you will see 150 acres of land, a good house and barns, 20 sheep, and 40 head of cattle. . . . You will see four mules, and a span of horses, two buggies, a double sleigh, and three buffalo-robes. He has drinked 'em all up—and 2 horse-rakes, a cultivator, and a thrashin'-machine" (146). Her sons "inherited their father's evil habits, and drink as bad as he duz; and the oldest girl has gone to the bad."

Dorlesky's cousin is in the "lunatick asylum." She had fallen on the street in a faint on a "brilin' hot" day while in New York buying millinary goods for her mother's store. She "was called drunk, and dragged off to a police court by a man who wus a animal in human shape. And he misused her in such a way, that she never got over the horror of what befell her—when she come to, to find herself at the mercy of a brute in a man's shape. She went into a melancholy madness, and wus sent to the asylum" (147).

One of Dorlesky's aunts was "molderin' in jail" for failing to tear up good sidewalks in front of her property to please the ward boss; another's property wasn't taxed until her circuit-riding husband died. "You see, Eliphalet's salary stopped when his breath did. And I s'pose mebby the law thought, seein' she was a havin' trouble, she might jest as well have a little more; so it taxed all the property it never had taxed a cent for before. But she had this to console her anyway,—that the law didn't forget her in her widowhood" (155).

Holley emphasizes again the physical vulnerability of women when the law "gives control of her body" to her husband. Aunt Drusilla Burpy was occasionally cross with her husband, Samantha supposed, because he insisted on a large family and left to her the entire care of the house and 11 children that had come along one year after another. Industrious, hardworking, and temperate, Drusilla's husband was "a master hand for wantin' to foller the laws of his country, as tight as laws could be follered." He wanted to follow the law that allows "moderate correction" of a man's wife, and "it was s'posed that he wanted to do his best for the law; and so, when he got to whippin' Drusilla, he would whip her *too* severe—he would be *too* faithful to it" (156–57; emphasis in original). To show that Drusilla was not as cross as he supposed, Samantha notes that though she outweighed him by 80 pounds and "might have whipped him if the law had been such," Drusilla too was law-abidin' and "never once whipped him in all the 17 years they lived together."

Though Holley tries to apply the same ironic topsy-turvy style to the issue of wife beating that she uses so effectively with other topics, this time her attempt is curious and disturbing. This time it doesn't ring true.

Then there was Abigail Burpy Flanders, married to a good-looking, law-abidin', high-headed man who had just one little eccentricity—"that man would lock up Abigail Burpy's clothes every time he got mad at her. Of course the law give her clothes to him; and knowin' it was one of the laws of the United States, she wouldn't have complained only when she had company. But it was mortifyin', and nobody could dispute it, to have company come, and nothin' to put on" (159).

Conjuring an image of a shivering Abigail waiting out the visitors' "neighborin'," a droll Samantha comments: "I'll bet that Abigail Flanders beat our old Revolutionary 4 mothers in thinkin' out new laws, when she lay round under stairs, and behind barrells, in her nightdress. . . . You see, when a man hides his wive's corset and petticoat, it is governin' without the 'consent of the governed.' And if you don't believe it, you ort to have peeked round them barrells, and seen Abigail's eyes. Why, they had hull reams of by-laws in 'em, and preambles, and 'declarations of independence' " (159–60).

In the chronicle of the Burpy women's sufferings, Holley touches on several concerns of both the WCTU's broad social agenda and the women's rights movement: the sanctioned practice of wife beating; the legal death of women who become wives; the total control of body, property, and children given over to husbands; the need for women guards of women prisoners to protect them from rape; taxation without representation; the ruin of families even unto the prostitution of daughters because of drunkenness. And in the process she emphasizes the interrelationship between temperance and suffrage, using language that includes "4 fathers," "4 mothers," and "4 people."

True to her calling, Samantha takes Dorlesky's "errent" to a senator who replies to her entreaties for her rights and for stomping the Whiskey Ring by commenting on Samantha's tatting and her hair, wondering whether bangs were going out of style. Government officials insult and trivialize women's petitions for the ordinary rights of citizenship by diverting the conversation to matters of accessories and portrayals of women as ethereal angels flying "in a floatin' fashion, up in the air smooth and serene." If you are bound to make angels of women, she says, "you ort to furnish a free, safe place for 'em to soar in. You ort to keep the angels from bein' meddled with, and bruised, and killed, etc." (214). Again turning to that self same "nature" so often used to justify women's "spear," Samantha delivers Dorlesky's message: "Dorlesky says you call wimmen angels, and you don't give 'em the rights of the lowest beasts that crawls upon the earth. And Dorlesky told me to tell you that she didn't ask the rights of a angel: she would be perfectly contented and proud if you would give her the rights of a dog—the assured political rights of a yeller dog" (215).

Among signs of the dog's higher political status are that it "don't have to pay taxes on its bone to a Government that withholds every right of citizenship from it"; it won't be hanged for breaking laws it had no part in making; "a dog hain't called undogly if it is industrious, and hunts quietly round for its bone to the best of its ability." Above all, "a dog don't have to listen to soul-sickening speeches from them that deny it freedom and justice—about its bein' a damosk rose, and a seraphine, when it knows it hain't: it knows, if it knows any thing, that it is a dog" (216).

In her discussions with President Chester Arthur, James G. Blaine, and other government officials, Samantha counters arguments of natural male superiority, biblical endorsement for male authority, unwillingness to tamper with the Constitution by changing the laws, and the like with parables that "fit the truth to weak comprehensions." Laws have been changed to lessen taxes on liquor so it can be sold cheaper and dealers will suffer no loss. Laws have been changed to cut down the money for Indian schools. They have accommodated selling at auction block the labor of inmates of poorhouses by the year to the highest bidder. In her "high ironical tone" Samantha laments, "A race of bein's, that make such laws as these, hadn't ort to be disturbed by wimmen meddlin' with 'em" (241).

Passed from one official to another to another, Dorlesky's "errents" meet with inaction. Some agree that they are just and right but they cannot do anything about it. Some admit that they want to drink everything they can and "they didn't want wimmen to vote, because they like to have the power in their own hands." One honest soul, lubricated by liquor, acknowledges that the legislators know who got them elected and couldn't vote against the liquor interests. And, of course they are awfully busy: "We senators and congressmen are so driven, and hard-worked we have no time to devote to the cause of Right and Justice" (231).

While in Washington, Samantha cites the jeering disrespect accorded a petition signed by thousands of women by legislators on the floor of Congress. She advocates compulsory education and visits the Peace Commission. She reflects on the lot of "black Africans" and Indians and even alludes to international copyright law. When she returns home ("the dearest word that was ever heard or sung"), she learns that yet another of Josiah's misguided schemes has resulted in his decision to give up political ambition after all.

In *Sweet Cicely* Holley does write her "temperance book." But as always, Samantha's "eppisodin'" ripples out from that central pebble and takes aim at the fallacy of denying women a direct voice in a society whose laws circumscribe their lives. Women need more weapons than pleading and begging. Samantha doesn't accept the flowery balderdash of Cicely's self-justifying executor that women, with their "dainty white hands" and "rosy smiles," are the real rulers of the world. People are not characters in a sentimental novel. "You see, he went on, as men used to went on, to females years ago. He forgot that that Alonzo and Melissa style of talkin' to wimmen had almost entirely gone out of fashion. And it was a good deal more stylish now to talk to wimmen as if they wuz human bein's, and men wuz too" (332).

Obedient to the Vision: Race

Holley was reluctant to write a book on racial issues. After all, though she and her family had been sympathetic to abolition, as a resident of rural upstate New York she had little direct experience with people of color. Her account of the genesis of *Samantha on the Race Problem* (1892) in "How I Wrote My First Books," reads like a spiritual calling. The call was issued by "two wise men," a clergyman from the South and one from the East who visited her home within two days of one another to ask her to write on "the race problem." Her pleas of ignorance on the subject elicited from them appeals to her sense of duty and pledges to help based on their own experience in the South. Seeking confirmation of their entreaties from "a higher light," Holley opened the Bible and rested her finger on three successive passages that she took as signs that she could not be "disobedient to the vision." That vision—of returning the former slaves to the "fertile valleys of the Nile"—was not a point of view that she or the clergymen had ever before advocated and seemed to take her by surprise. However, she felt compelled to write by "a stronger power than myself."[10]

So, emboldened by spiritual guidance and secular zeal for reform, she set out to "wrap her humor round the argument." Her lofty ideas exposing past injustices, current inequities, and continuing indignities must be seen, however, within the context of her time and limitations. Embedded in the language and images she uses to call attention to the pain of racial bigotry are patronizing racial stereotypes that expose the dated nature of her discourse.

In "The Story of My Life" she describes a trip she had taken to Virginia many years before where she witnessed signs that "Freedom and Liberty were beginning their work." She points to the sight of a woman ploughing on her homestead, where "her hard labor would be her own. She did not fear the visit of a slave buyer to look her over as he would a horse or cow and put a price upon her." Nor did she fear that her children ("wooly headed little urchins") would be torn from her arms and sold. Slowly, "Liberty and Justice are grinding away the results of slavery. And both the white and black race[s] are emerging into a truer freedom."[11]

On that same trip she visited and admired "the colored school at Hampton" from which Booker T. Washington had graduated. Holley praised the school's mission, but in terms that jolt the modern sensibility, when she notes a workshop "where I saw civilization at work with barbarism and turning out good material too." Her way of complimenting the black man who carried her bags, "so good natured and helpful," was to liken him to Kipling's Water Carrier: "For all his dirty hide / He was white, alas white inside." Of the "old negro mammy" Rhoda who used to work for her as housemaid, Holley said that "during her stay the rappings were often heard in our home. She must have been mediumistic, and was so simple and natural and so near to nature that she might have apprehended things that those more highly civilized were ignorant of."[12]

In several of Holley's books, Samantha's observations touching on race and ethnicity reveal both sympathetic insight into injustice and expedient pandering to racist or nativist stereotype. For example, at various times she engages the treatment of Native Americans by the U.S. government. In *Samantha at the Centennial* Samantha advises President Ulysses S. Grant on many subjects, including "Lo, the poor Injun." To his reply of "Darn Lo, anyway," she admonishes the posture that noble Uncle Sam has taken "a settin' down on the Injun race, a tryin' to choke 'em to death" (403). To Grant's defense that Samuel has "to take that posture or be scalped," Samantha counters: "If Samuel would let *me* pick out postures for him, I would have him stand up so far above Lo—in mercy, and justice, and patience, and truth,—that he couldn't reach up to his scalp; and standin' up on that height, he might deal less in glass beads, and more in common honesty" (403; emphasis in original).

In *Sweet Cicely* Samantha voices sarcastic disdain of the government official's explanation of the "constant pressure of hard work" attending legislators' efforts to ensure that liquor dealers suffer no loss, that money for Indian schools is reduced, that Chinese are sent "back into heathendom" with appropriate biblical texts, and other pressing concerns. The official instructs Samantha in a "proud tone": ". . . we men don't begrudge labor if we can advance measures of economy. You see, it was taking sights of money just to Christianize and civilize Injuns—savages. Why, the idea was worse than useless, it wus perfectly ruinous to the Indian agents. For if, through those schools, the Indians had got to be self-supporting and intelligent and Christians, why, the agents couldn't buy their wives and daughters for a yard of calico, or get them drunk, and buy a horse for a glass bead, and a farm for a pocket lookin'-glass" (231–32).

Though Holley criticizes the official treatment of Indians, she also resorts to unflattering stereotypes when Samantha tackles a different subject. Later on in her trip to Washington, D.C., Samantha feels she must visit the Peace Commission to "make some arrangements with 'em to not have any more wars." Furthermore, "as I told Sally, 'We might jest as well call ourselves Injuns and savages at once, if we had to keep up this most savage and brutal trait of theirn'" (254).

With regard to foreigners and immigrants, Holley is at once tolerant of difference and willing to assign traits of weakness based on ethnic affiliation. In *Sweet Cicely* Holley disparages xenophobia by putting its articulation in the mouth of myopic Josiah, who thinks there shouldn't be anybody in America "only jest Methodists." He would "run every poor Irishman and Chinaman out of the country" because of their poverty. The Chinese are "heathen" who "work too cheap." If he had his way, he would send the "hull caboodle" (with Chinese, Irish, Catholics, Jews, and so on) out of the country. The Statue of Liberty can light their way out. Samantha doubts "that wus what she wus there for." Josiah does not concede the point.

> I s'posed it wus a gift from a land that helped us to liberty and prosperity when we needed 'em as bad as the Irishmen and Chinamen do to-day; and I s'posed that torch that wus lit for us by others' help, we should be willin' and glad to have it shine on the dark cross-roads of others.
>
> "Wall, it hain't meant for no such purpose: it is to light up *our* land and *our* waters. That's what *she's* there for." (119; emphasis in original)

But when it comes to arguing for woman suffrage, Holley uses both the justice and expediency arguments. The latter often embraced nativism by invoking the image of women (usually middle- to upper-class educated white women) casting ballots to counter the votes of immigrants and "low, ignorant coots who'd probably think the franchise wuz some kind of meat stew." In *My Opinions* Samantha claims that even if women don't read about the laws, "they'll know as much as some other folks do."

> "I have seen men voters. . . . whose study into national affairs didn't wear on 'em enough to kill 'em at all. I have seen voters," says I with another cuttin' look at [Josiah], "that didn't know as much as their wives did. . . . I have seen Irish voters, whose intellects wasn't tiresome to carry round, and whose knowledge concernin' public affairs wasn't so good as it was about rum, and who would sell their votes for a drink of whiskey, and keep it up all day, votin' and drinkin' and then drinkin' and votin', and I guess wimmen won't do any worse." (229–30)

When Holley turned her attentions to the "black Africans," it was to decry the abomination of slavery, rejoice in the emancipation, and struggle for solutions to complicated issues of education, land ownership, the franchise, and so forth brought on by manumission. In *My Opinions* Samantha declares that only now could she write about "Wimmen's Rites" because heretofore she had been busy with husband and small children, and "the subject of black African slavery also wearin' on me, and a mortgage of 200 and 50 dollars on the farm." The "black African also bein' liberated about the same time of the mortgage," she could now set her shoulder blades to the wheel and proceed. Holley satirizes those who had defended slavery when Samantha must endure the arrogant boasting of Jeremiah Gansey, whose self-described great work, "Logical Reveries on the Beauties' of Slavery," he claimed had been "devoured by the masses" and precipitated the Civil War.

And, as had others in the women's rights movement, Holley drew comparisons between the condition of blacks and women when she likened race slavery to wife slavery. Samantha points out to Josiah that given the way he talks, you'd think that a woman could do only one thing—either vote or marry. And that if she could live any other way than by marrying, she couldn't be persuaded to sign on for that institution.

> . . . if marryin' is such a dreadful nice thing for wimmen I don't see what you are afraid of. You men act kinder guilty about it, and I don't wonder at it, for take a bad husband, and their haint no kind of slavery to be compared to wife slavery. . . . Figurin' accordin' to the closest rule of

arithmetic, there are at least one-third mean, dissopated, drunken men in the world, and they most all have wives, and let them tread on these wives ever so hard, if they only tread accordin' to law, she can't escape. And suppose she tries to escape, blood-hounds haint half so bitter as public opinion on a women [*sic*] that parts with her husband, chains and handcuffs haint to be compared to her pride, and her love for her children, and so she keeps still, and suffers agony enough to make four first class martyrs. Field slaves have a few hours for rest at night, and a hope, to kinder boy them up, of gettin' a better master. But the wife slave has no hope of a change of masters, and let him be ever so degraded and brutal is at his mercy day and night. (95–96)

According to law, the wife is the husband's property, just as the slave is the master's property, and each must hope for the noble, generous protector and avoid the mean, cowardly tyrant. Interestingly, though Holley makes this connection in her book devoted to women's rights, she does not take up that theme in her book devoted to race.

Like women who can find no refuge of justice in the law, blacks are not patronizingly protected but rather are powerless before the laws that discriminate against them. "One of the laws enacted of late in the South permits a white man to kill a black man for a crime committed aginst his honor, and if the white man commits the same crime and the black man takes the same revenge, he is killed at once accordin' to law—one man liberated with rejoicings, the other shot down like a dog. Do you say the black man is more ignorant? That is a bad plea" (134).

Meanwhile, in assessing the language Holley uses to express her ideas, it is important to remember that the nomenclature referring to racial groups (ethnic groups, gender identification, and people with disabilities for that matter) changes over time. Therefore, holding a previous age to the standards of current usage is inappropriate. Still, the word *nigger* has always been pejorative when used by whites. Though Holley clearly expresses sympathy for the plight and regard for the person, Samantha repeatedly refers to blacks as *niggers* in a manner probably consistent with the time but charged with offensive meaning. Only in *Samantha on the Race Problem* does Holley put the word in quotation marks (and that is done inconsistently), signifying an awareness of its connotation and a reluctance for the sympathetic persona of Samantha to be identified with its demeaning import.

However reluctantly, Holley determined to write about the "Negro Question" during Reconstruction in the South and made that the center of *Samantha on the Race Problem*, which was issued for the subscription market. When it was reprinted in 1894 for the popular market, the publishers changed the title to *Samantha Among the Colored Folks*. The book opens with Josiah's cousin John Richard arriving, with a satchel of Bibles and tracts in hand, for an unexpected visit. He has been raising money for a freedman's school[13] and meetinghouse in the South and warns of a brooding storm of Reconstruction that could lead to another war. Samantha and Josiah, with no firsthand knowledge at this point, sit in the North listening to Cousin John's cautionary tale about the South that includes his regrettable conclusion that the two races cannot live together harmoniously. Whites, he says, will never look upon blacks as their equals. And, in an astonishing prediction of black fertility, he predicts that whites will be outnumbered by 1 million people in 20 years.

Based on his observations, he argues that gradual emancipation that gave time for education and Christianity to do its groundwork might have been a better course than immediate freedom. Because that had not happened, he suggests that the government send the young and healthy former slaves back to Africa where they could found a new republic that would not have prejudices and antagonism of race that are smoldering in the United States.

Josiah listens to his cousin, disdainful of Southerners' treatment of blacks but claiming that it is "none of our business." Holley foreshadows the enormous personal, emotional loss the Allens will experience when to Samantha's assertion that "the cause of eternal truth is *always* our bizness," Josiah replies: "There hain't no earthly possibility that this nigger question can affect us one way or another; there haint no way for it to" (57; emphasis in original).

The location shifts to the South when their son Thomas Jefferson, his wife Maggie, their newborn son, and daughter Snow go to Georgia for the winter because of Maggie's health. All in the family become ill, so Samantha and Josiah join them to help out. This provides the immediate experience with race relations that had been unavailable to them in Jonesville where, Samantha acknowledges, she had never neighbored with anyone "darker complexioned than myself." They learn that Thomas and Maggie's neighbors despised the "idee" of schools for blacks and seemed to look upon blacks "as Josiah and me looked onto our dairy, though mebby not quite so favorably, for there wuz one young yearlin' heifer and one three-year-old Jersey that I always said knew enough to vote" (259).

The Allens grow increasingly fond of the family nurse, Genevieve, and her fiancé Victor, both of whom look white but are of mixed race. Holley weaves into the narrative long accounts of mixed blood, betrayal, servant and master who are really brothers. She counters the virtue, industry, and intelligence of Victor, Genevieve, and their friend Felix with descriptions of a family of lazy, ignorant, amoral blacks prone to the secrecy, lying, and stealing taught them by "the [slave] system under which they wuz born and nurtured." Again the limits of Holley's view are illustrated by Samantha's language when she describes the granddaughter in the family: "She wuz rather pretty for a full-blooded African. A empty-headed, gigglin', utterly depraved study in black" (156).

Through the people she meets and the stories they tell, Samantha comes to believe that the messages dinned into the ears of blacks—that Christianity, education and merit will win you the prizes of life—were not true. Blacks who by industry had prospered a little were run off or lynched. An energetic, intelligent, Christian black man, Victor runs the plantation affairs of his white half-brother, who exploits Victor's labor and denies him kinship and basic human respect. Victor is the leader of the colonization movement. At the book's end, all the plans are finally in place; he is to marry Genevieve the next day and they are to leave for Africa. As Victor holds Samantha's beloved granddaughter Snow on his lap, a bullet shot from outside the house crashes through Snow's breast, killing her. Knowing it was meant for him, Victor confronts his masked antagonists who insist he give up his plans or die. He dies blessing them. Genevieve receives an inheritance from her long-departed white father, Victor's friend Felix takes over as leader, and they form a new republic in Africa called Victor.

Both Samantha and Josiah had rhapsodized about the beauty, demeanor, and intelligence of their beloved Snow. The final image of the narrative finds the grieving Samantha back home in Jonesville, sitting on the stoop at sunset enjoying the bucolic serenity of nature when a light breeze falls across her forehead and cheek "like a soft, consolin' little hand." By sacrificing a character so important to Samantha in order to make her point about racial hatred, Holley underscores the magnitude of her commitment to racial justice. And to the notion that the race question is not just a regional issue and does indeed affect everyone.

On the other hand, while Samantha had initially proposed education and Christianity as the answer to the race conundrum, she is gradually persuaded by Victor's position. The conclusion that race relations are at such an impasse that the only solution is recolonization in Africa seems at the very least impractical. However well-meaning the impulse and idyllic the description of the new republic, this is not a comprehensive remedy that discharges Uncle Sam's responsibilities to a previously enslaved people.[14]

Holley does not exonerate those who have not owned slaves from the exploitation of the vulnerable by the rich and powerful. Those consigned to piecework in the cities are "white slaves" who make shirts for 5¢ each, and "sign their contracts with their blood" (84). "Col. Seybert drove and swore, and threatened his [freed] negroes as his great-uncle Wiggins drove the white operatives in his big Northern factory, kept them at starvation wages, and piled up his money-bags over the prostrate forms of gaunt, overworked men and women, and old young children, who earned his money out of their own hopeless youth . . . Northern cupidity and avarice, Southern avarice and cupidity, equally ugly in God's sight, so we believe" (119).

When the racial issue is linked with suffrage, Holley for the first time suggests a limited suffrage. It is significant that only in this book does she propose any educational requirement to exercise the franchise. In cataloging the conditions of Reconstruction South, Samantha had supposed that part of the blame lay with immediate emancipation. Because blacks had been kept deliberately ignorant for the purposes of the oppressor, they needed to be gradually trained and educated so that they could ably conduct their own affairs and guide their own futures. Because black men had been given the right to vote when former slaves were made citizens of the United States through the Fourteenth Amendment[15] and because that could not now "be taken from them for a long time without a war followin'," a logical step would be to extend the suffrage to women. "There is one thing that might be *tried*—give the ballot to the white women of the South, and to the black women too, if they can come up to the standpoint of intelligence. Let a certain amount of education and intelligence be the qualification to the ballot" (165; emphasis in original).

The assumption, no doubt, is that most white women and some few black women (such as Genevieve) would qualify. Through Samantha, Holley proposes an elitist view with educated men and women on the one hand and the illiterates of the South and the "loafer rabble in Northern cities"—the lower classes—on the other. Though outraged by the consequences of blind bigotry and humanely sympathetic with the plight of the emancipated but generally uneducated blacks, Holley forgoes genuine efforts at full integration into society by endorsing at least temporary solutions in colonization and implicitly supports southern women whose interests lie in keeping whites in power.[16]

As with *Sweet Cicely* and the temperance cause, extended sketches in *Samantha on the Race Question* are unrelated to the central theme, and they in fact carry the crux of the humor. For the most part, Holley's humor is not "wrapped around" the race argument. Long sections recounting wrongs done to blacks and the need for education read like essays. Only occasionally does Samantha's folksy voice seem to break through. Even the dialect and misspelling are mostly abandoned. For the most part race is a serious topic treated seriously, even melodramatically, with occasional flashes of repartee and humor emerging in sketches involving visiting relatives prone to hysterical fits or musical inundation, Josiah's scheme to become a delegate to the Pan American Congress,[17] speculations about the wives of the Old Testament prophets, and discussion about potential tombstone inscriptions.

This time when Samantha and Josiah return from their winter's journey to peaceful domesticity in Jonesville, they return with heavy hearts—and with the certain knowledge that Josiah's doctrine that "if you let an evil alone it will do you no harm—wuz all broke down and crushed to pieces" (365).

The Cause of Eternal Justice: Religion

Marietta Holley took religion seriously. As mentioned in an earlier chapter, she was a member of one of the Baptist congregations in Jefferson County, having converted at age 16 during a revival meeting. In her autobiography, she remembered the considerable emotional effort that her testimony required of one so naturally timid: "When I united with the church, and Heavens knows I was in earnest, it was almost a physical impossibility for me to rise and tell about the struggles and victories of my inner life. So hard was it indeed that when I tried to do what others did and rise up, it would seem as if the seat would come up with me. It seemed too sacred and too much of a secret between my soul and the All Highest to talk about to brother and sister mortals."[18]

Holley believed in direct divine guidance as illustrated by her habit of starting the day by holding the Bible in her left hand and opening it with her right. "The verse upon which her right thumb rested was the law for the day."[19]

She also believed in the presence of departed spirits and the efficacy of Ouija boards to communicate on a spiritual plane. Though distrustful of professional mediums, she was intrigued by the mysteries of otherworldly contact that she could not explain in other than spiritualistic terms.

Holley's literary persona shares her fascination with spiritualism but has chosen a different church. Samantha never tires of reading *Foxe's Book of Martyrs*, and endorses the presence of departed souls in *Sweet Cicely* and other works. In *Samantha vs. Josiah, Being the Story of a Borrowed Automobile and What Came of It* (1906), nearly the entire book is given over to stories of the occult and psychic experiences, most of which Holley had collected over the years from her friends and which later appear in her autobiography.

Holley recognized not only the power of personal religious faith but the influence of the church as a central institution of moral authority in society. The church, however, has not always been right in the cause of Eternal Justice. Holley exposed religious hypocrisy and gender inequity as proclaimed both from the pulpits of churches and the cracker barrels of the general store. Though personally devoted to the church and the Bible, Holley satirized the use of scripture to uphold male supremacy and deny women a place in the hierarchy of the church. She often used religious allusions to illuminate issues outside that circumscribed sphere, among them history's treatment of women, options of direct and indirect influence for women, the double standard, the perceived universality of language, and economic dependence of women on men.

A faithful sister in the Methodist Meetin' House of Jonesville, Samantha preaches religious tolerance:

> I despise the idee of folks bein' so sot on their own meetin' housen. Their is enough worldly things for neighbors to fight about, such as hens, and the schoolmarm, without takin' what little religion they have got and go to peltin' each other with it.
>
> Sposen Baptists do love water better'n they do dry land? What of it? If my Baptist brethren feel any better to baptise thierselves in the Atlantic ocian, it haint none of my business. (*Opinions*, 69)

A stark exception to this tolerance lay in her attitude toward the Mormons.[20] Like Artemus Ward and other nineteenth-century humorists, Holley lashes out at the Mormon Church, particularly the practice of polygamy. She devotes an entire long poem, *The Lament of the Mormon Wife* (1880), to the fate of the "own true wife" eventually displaced in the heart of her beloved by the other wives that followed. In *My Wayward Pardner* Samantha launches into a nearly 70-page diatribe against the "nefariousness and heniousness" of Mormonism precipitated by the oft-wed Elder Judas Wart's proposal of marriage to her. Seeing that Samantha was outraged at his "infamous offer" to be "sealed" to him, Elder Wart hastens to say that he "meant it in a religious way." Samantha counters: "Wall! I'll scald you in a religious way. . . . But I'll bet a cent you won't never want to be scalded agin as long as you live" (407). Samantha and the Elder try to convince one another of the rightness of their respective doctrines, to no avail. As Samantha explains to the Elder, the worst sin of Mormonism is the practice of men having many wives. "And I can tell you, and tell you plain, that I have laid awake nights a thinkin' over what my sect has endured a settin' under that Mormon church. . . . For of all the sufferin's my sect has suffered from the hands of man, this doctrine of polygamy is the very crown, the crown of thorns. Why, the rights and wrongs of my sect has for years been held nearer to my heart than any earthly object, exceptin' my Josiah. Other wrongs and woes have spilte earth for her time and agin, but this destroys her hope of heaven" (419–20).

Holley mines the logic of orthodoxy for the inconsistencies and injustices it gives up regarding the place of women and men in God's universe. Samantha expands and subverts conventional interpretations by putting a different spin on familiar Bible stories. In a sketch about the wives of the Old Testament prophets in *Samantha Among the Colored Folks*, her conjectures suggest that their function was one that has remained constant over historical time in society's eyes: healer and nurturer, comforter and guardian, workhorse and hostess. While Samantha honors the old prophets, she feels sorry for their wives. "Not a word do we hear about them, and it makes me feel bad to see my sect so overlooked and brought down to nort" (311). She imagines that old Miss Daniel and Miss Zekiel and Miss Maleky and the rest, "had a tough time on't." As if it weren't enough to see their beloved men "wanderin' about in sheepskin and goatskin, and bein' afflicted, and destitute, and tormented," those old females probably "jest wrastled round with household cares and left them old men as free as they could" to holler "Woe! woe! to this wicked city! etc." Samantha catalogs the chores she suspects those women performed, including brushing the prophet's goatskin before he set off on a "prophesying trip" and bucking him up when he returned from a bad day at the persecutions.

> But who thinks anything of these old female wimmen's labors and sufferin's? Nobody.
> Who thinks of their martyrdom, their efforts in the good cause, and the help they gin the old male prophets? Nobody, not one.

> I spoze the account of these things bein' writ down by males and translated by 'em makes a difference; it's sort o' naterel to stand up for your own sect.
>
> But folks ort to own up, male or female; and them old females ort to have justice done 'em. (316–17)

Because women's contributions have not customarily existed in the political, religious, *public* sphere, they have not been acknowledged in any historically significant way. She understates the motive, but Samantha certainly understands that women have been invisible in history because men have written the books and decided what was important to record.[21]

By creating a hypothetical circumstance from the Bible that transcends any fixed time period, Holley underscores the nature of Scripture as stories recorded at a time and place in history, rather than divine inspirations to be taken literally. Scripture has been self-servingly interpreted to uphold male supremacy. In one of her periodic discussions with a government official, who not incidentally reveals his ignorance of the text by referring to the book of "Lilliputions," Samantha refutes his contention that "the Bible teaches man's supremacy, man's absolute power and might and authority" (*Sweet Cicely*, 223). She points to the power of Eve while decrying the destructiveness of indirect influence:

> Why, in the very first chapter, the Bible tells how man was jest turned right round by a woman. It teaches how she not only turned man right round to do as she wanted him to, but turned the hull world over.
> That hain't nothin I approve of: I don't speak of it because I like the idee. That wuzn't done in a open, honorable manner, as I believe things should be done. No: Eve ruled by indirect influence,—the 'gently influencing men' way, that politicians are so fond of. And she jest brought ruin and destruction onto the hull world by it. (*Cicely*, 223)

Samantha goes on to applaud later women who "didn't act meachin', and tempt, and act indirect": "A few years later, after men and wimmen grew wiser, when we hear of wimmen ruling Israel openly and honestly, like Miriam, Deborah, and other likely old 4 mothers, why, things went on better" (*Cicely*, 223).

Holley often attacks the double standard of behavior required for men and women. In a chapter called "The Male Magdalene" in *Samantha vs. Josiah* she had used the technique of simple reversal to revise the story of the fallen woman. Handsome Nelt Chawgo's head is turned by the sweet nothin's whispered in his ear by Angerose Wilds, a "dashin' young woman" who has come into an inheritance, "sows her wild oats," and leaves. The long and the short of it is that modest and moral Nelt becomes a fallen man, a "ruint feller," a "he-hussy." The scandal nearly rents the town to twain with folks arguing over whose fault it is. To Deacon Henzy's adherence to the "old well-established doctrine" that it was sin in a woman but not in a man, a WCTU lecturer who had come to town retorted: "The idee of thinkin' that the same sin when committed by a man and a woman ort to be laid entirely onto the party that is in the law classed with lunaticks and idiots . . . that hain't good logic. If a woman is a fool she hadn't ort to be expected to have her brain tapped and run wisdom and morality, and if she is a lunatick she might be expected to cut up and act" (309–10). Ever-megum Samantha thinks "they ort to carry the pail between 'em." It all turns out in the end when Angerose learns of Nelt's status, repents for her hurtful ways, and promises to marry Nelt and thereby "make an honest man of him."

Sometimes Holley's ammunition is found in familiar biblical stories. Samantha's rendering of the story of Abraham, Sarah, and Hagar in *Samantha at the Centennial*, for example, exposes the hypocrisy of unshared blame and connects sexual misdeeds by males with the reaping of rewards. Samantha declares that she "never contended that wimmen was perfect, far from it," and she acknowledges that women could be "meaner than pusly about some things." But in justice, equal rights, and "a fair dividin' of the burdens of life," women have not fared well.

> Now in the year one, when Adam and Eve eat that apple, jest as quick as Adam swallowed it—probably he most choked himself with the core, he was in such a awful hurry to get his mouth clear, so he could lay the blame onto Eve. . . .
> But thank fortin, . . . Eternal Goodness, which is God, is forever on the side of Right. And Adam and Eve—as any two ort to be who sin together—got turned out of Eden, side by side, out of the same gate, into the same wilderness. . . . (*Centennial*, 179–80)

But when Abraham and Hagar sinned together, only Hagar was sent off to the wilderness. Wishing that she had "lived neighbor" to him at the time so she could counsel the old patriarch, Samantha reasons that Abraham was not doing the fair and honorable thing by sending Hagar and their baby out into the desert with nothing but one loaf of bread and a bottle of water between them and death. What is "sass for the goose, ort to be sass for the gander." Samantha acknowledges that old Abraham no doubt felt the pressure from his wife Sarah: "And I persume Sarah kep' at him all the time; . . . kep' him awake nights a twittin' him about her, and askin' him to start her off. I persume Sarah acted meaner than pusly."

But from that time to this, take it between the Abrahams and the Sarahs of this world, the Hagars have fared hard, and the Abrahams have got along first rate; the Hagars have been turned out into the desert to die there, and the Abrahams that ruined 'em, have increased in flocks and herds; are thought a sight of and are high in the esteem of wimmen. Seems as though the more Hagars they fit out for the desert business, the more feathers it is in their cap . . . till some get completely feathered out; then they send 'em to Congress, and think a sight on 'em. (*Centennial*, 182–83)

For this state of affairs, Samantha blames women because they wink at the sins of men, while "not a wink can you ever git out of them about our sins. . . . We ort to require as much purity and virtue in them, as they do in us, and stop winkin'" (183).

Samantha Among the Brethren

As with temperance in *Sweet Cicely* and race in *Samantha Among the Colored Folks*, Holley offers extended assessment of the church in *Samantha Among the Brethren* (1890). As is customary, after the preface declaring the theme, it takes nearly half the book (and accounts of a couple of sets of sentimental people who need to be put right by Samantha) before Samantha actually engages the topic. The preface is all about language and women. Samantha opens with biblical language ("Again it come to pass, in the fulness of time . . .") and then moves on to secular speech and the inappropriateness of the perceived universality of the pronoun *he*. When Josiah sees Samantha take her inkstand from the mantle, he asks what she aims to "tackle" now. Answering "The Cause of Eternal Justice," Samantha amplifies the nature of her task: "I lay out in petickuler to tackle the Meetin' House. She is in the wrong on't, and I want to set her right" (vii).

Josiah takes considerable umbrage at this atypical usage and claims the Meetin' House "hadn't ort to be called she—it is a he." When asked on what grounds he makes that claim, Josiah confidently proclaims, "Because it stands to reason." That's a compelling argument, of course, but Samantha reminds him the Meetin' House is called the "Mother Church"—and the Bible refers to "the Church bein' arrayed like a bride for her husband."

Samantha's "petickuler" complaint about the Meetin' House is that it "hain't a-actin' right about wimmen." Jesus was born of a woman, and women have worked hard for the church generation after generation. But the church has not treated women well. Women's exclusion from the governance of the church is wrong and Samantha is going to "write out jest what I think about it." Samantha and Josiah serve and volley their respective pronouns to refer to the church until he abruptly concludes the discussion with "Don't be too hard on *him*." Then he does what he always does when Samantha has boxed him into a logical corner—leaves and shuts the door behind him before she can say another word.[22]

When Samantha does finally arrive at her topic, she "episodes" on the rights withheld from women of the church and the spurious reasoning that accompanies the blanket denial of those rights. Holley places these grievances in the context of the 1888 General Conference of the Methodist Episcopal Church, which had refused to seat duly elected women delegates on the grounds that admission of women was not in accordance with the constitutional provisions of the church embodied in the Restrictive Rules. A special investigative commission was appointed, but it eventually reported adversely on admission of the women delegates, one of whom was Holley's friend Frances Willard.

In a publisher's index to *Samantha Among the Brethren* six of the arguments—three for and three against admission—are cited. Those speaking against admission relied either upon strict adherence to what they argued was the intention of the rules or upon ludicrous distinctions in definition. Perhaps most hairsplitting of the opponents was the Reverend James Buckley, who claimed that the word *layman* was created to indicate a separate class from clergyman. Because a separate class called *clergywoman* did not exist, there was no need for a separate class called *laywoman*. Therefore, *layman* means men who are not clergymen. He goes on to cite Lincoln's *Gettysburg Address* and the famous "of the people, by the people, and for the people" phrase. The dictionary, he reasons, would say that *people* means men, women, and children. But, clearly, Lincoln did not mean for women and children to take part in the government of the nation.

The Reverend Theodore Flood argued for admission on the grounds that the right of suffrage, which women had possessed for 16 years, carried with it the right to hold office. The Reverend A. B. Leonard likewise favored seating women because women had always been regarded as "laymen" in the practical work and administration of the church: they pay quarterage, contribute to benevolent collections, pray, and testify. They are tried by the same process as men and subject to the same penalties of suspension and expulsion. There are only two orders of the church—clergy and laity.

Not surprisingly, Holley gives the Buckley logic to Josiah and the Flood-Leonard rationale to Samantha. The sisters of the Methodist Meetin' House have a "conendrum" they have to "grapple onto." The church has fallen into disrepair, and the minister's salary hasn't been paid. The women want to refurbish the building and replenish the pastor. They ask the "male pardners" to help in this project. The men want to dreadfully, of course, but to a man they find themselves too busy just then to offer assistance of any sort. While their unwillingness to contribute time, energy, and muscle is irritating, their refusal to contribute "cash money" is potentially crippling. The women decide to give a big fair, selling things to raise money. But "it wuz a fearful tuff job we had took onto ourselves, for we had got to make all the things to sell out of what we could get hold of, for, of course, our husbands all kep the money purses in their own hands, as the way of male pardners is" (243). Josiah is notoriously "clost with his money," and so offers only 10¢ to the cause. This is particularly galling to Samantha because he has sold a horse she raised by hand for $215, and she expected at least $15 in response to her request.

The other "pardners" are equally generous. Samantha reasons that there "hain't a question a-comin' up before that Conference that is harder to tackle than this plasterin' and the conendrum that is up before us Jonesville wimmen how to raise 300 dollars out of nuthin', and to make peace in a meetin' house where anarky is now rainin' down" (249). The women spend their time pulling and tugging at heavy pews, standing on barrels, and scraping walls laboring for the church. The men check in at the editor's office periodically to learn whether the Conference has decided that women are too "weak to set."

According to the Articles, it is acceptable, even welcome, for women to labor, even to do *all* the work of fixing up the "old house," but when it comes to "the hard and arjuous duties of drawin' saleries with 'em [men], or settin' up on Conferences with 'em, why there a line had to be drawn, wimmen must not be permitted to strain herself in no such ways—nor resk the tender delicacy of her nature, by settin' in a meetin' house es a delegate by the side of a man once a year. It wuz too resky" (244–45).

To secure the necessary money, the women resort to hard work (seating pairs of trousers for a few cents each), sacrifice (contributing an item of great sentimental value to be sold), and even deceit (egg money, butter money, dried apple money kept back from husbands). Holley contends that women are unpaid labor dependent on the generosity of husbands or fathers in a society that values both money and independence.

Women are subject to the same punishments of the church, but those sanctions are meted out only by the male brethren and differently depending on one's "sect." The Meetin' House hauled Sister Henn up and punished her mightily for laughing during a meeting. Deacon Widrig, meanwhile, is punished lightly for his transgressions because, Samantha says, he contributed both money and hard cider to the brethren. "Men are judged by their peers, but women never are" (231).

Holley points to the ironies that derive from the rationale that women should not appear or speak in public. People horrified at the idea of sending female delegates to the Conference have no difficulty praising women who sing in public to raise money to buy the paper for the church walls. Mahala Gowdey had raised her "sulferine" voice and put on "sights and sights of quavers" at the public concert.

> But they all said that wuz a *very* different thing.
> And sez I, "How different?" She wuz a yellin' in public for the good of the Methodist Mettin' House (it wuz her voice that drawed the big congregatin, we all know). And them wimmen delegates would only have to 'yea' and 'nay' in a still small voice for the good of the same. I can't see why it would be so much more indelicate and unbecomin' in them—and sez I, "they would have bonnets and shawls on, and she that wuz Mahala had on a low neck and short sleeves." (247)

As discussed in chapter 2, Holley had addressed the issue of women speaking in public via her interview with Horace Greeley in *My Opinions*. Proposing that a woman should speak "if she has got anything to say for God and humanity," Samantha also endorses the idea of women being preachers in God's church.[23] Though she does not return so directly to the issue of women clergy in *Samantha Among the Brethren,* Holley takes on both the claim of differential intelligence between men and women and the convoluted intricacies of textual interpretation that would deny women a place in the leadership of the church.

Josiah tries to explain to Samantha that the word *laymen* doesn't include women. It turns out that it *always* means women when they can help men (vote them to church office, etc.). And when it is used in "a punishin' and condemnatory sense, or in the case of work and so fourth, but when it comes to settin' up in high places, or drawin' sallerys, or anything else difficult, it alweys means men" (255). Samantha dryly suggests that it also means women when "scrubbin' is concerned, and drowdgin' round." Then Holley links the sacred with the secular worlds by showing that the same kind of logic is used to deny women the rights of citizenship as is offered to restrict their voice in the church. Samantha says, in "fearful dry axents, almost pesky ones," that it takes "quite a knack" to decipher the gender application of such terminology.

> "That is so," sez Josiah. "It takes a man's mind to grapple with it; wimmen's minds are too weak to tackle it. It is jest es it is with that word 'men' in the Declaration of Independence. Now that word 'men', in that Declaration, means men some of the time, and some of the time men and wimmen both. It means both sexes when it relates to punishment, taxin' property, obeyin' the laws strictly, etc., etc., and then it goes right on the very next minute and means men only, as to wit, namely, votin, takin' charge of public matters, makin' laws, etc.
> "I tell you it takes deep minds to foller on and see jest to a hair where the division is made. It takes statesmanship.
> "Now take that claws, 'All men are born free and equal.'
> "Now half of that means men, and the other half men and wimmen. Now to understand them words perfect you have got to divide the tex. 'Men are born.' That means men and wimmen both . . . nobody can dispute that. Then comes the next claws, 'Free and equal.' Now that means men only—anybody with one eye can see that. . . ." (256–57)

The days go on, the women scrapin' old wallpaper and the men explicating doctrine. Suddenly, the men burst through the Meetin' House doors to announce the news that women have been appointed deaconesses. The women stop mopping to learn that if they were in fact unmarried females, they could enjoy the privilege of "workin' [their] hull life for the meetin' house, with a man to direct [their] movements and take charge . . . and tell [them] what to do, from day to day and from hour to hour" (264). They would not be able to serve the sacraments or pass the collection box, these being "hard and arjueus dutys" belonging to the male deaconship . . . "their own one pertickiler work, that wimmen can't infringe upon." But they could relieve the sick and suffering, sit up with smallpox patients, tend to the poor, and so forth. Not wanting to "curtail the holy rights of wimmen," the men would see to it that nothing really changed, that they would go on "in the same sure old way of superentendin' [wimmen's] movements, guardin' her weaker footsteps, and bossin' her round generally" (267).

At the end of the narrative, the men again burst triumphantly into the church—at a critical papering moment for the women balanced precariously on barrels—to announce that it had been decided that "women was too weak and fraguile to set on the Conference." The men leave in self-congratulatory high spirits. The women, perspiring from hard labor and grateful at that point to "set down on anything" resume the task "with giddy heads and strainin' armpits" of tackling the meetin' house.

Holley's point is clear. To claim the rights and privileges denied them by the church, women must have voting power on governing conferences; they must maintain some measure of economic independence; they must be judged by their peers and by the same standard applied to the brethren; and they must be allowed to speak publicly without fear of being labeled "unwomanly." In the religious sphere as in the secular sphere, women have not been accorded equal human rights.

Chapter Five

Etcetery, Etcetery, Etcetery: The Later Works

After publication of *Samantha on the Race Problem* in 1892, Holley had explored most of the themes she would articulate. Subsequent works provided variations on or repetitions of those themes. In fact, in some cases, she commits self-plagiarism, lifting passages from her earlier works, changing the names, and soaring on as if it were the first time around. She revisits and rehashes themes of temperance, women's rights, fashion, and spiritualism while more fully engaging issues of war, imperialism, the relationship between labor and capital, white slave traffic, and children's rights. As ever, Josiah's harebrained schemes need to be "squenched," but the tone of exchanges between the devoted "pardners" is sporadically more contentious and less good humored. Her patience sorely tested by now, Samantha tells him on one occasion to "shet up." On another, she views a scheme with "cold mockery." Still, amid much that is "tejus" and worn out in these later works, Holley continued to offer the periodic gem that sparkled in its transformation of a current event, trend, or exhibit into a folksy jewel of social satire.

Continuing the travel motif, Samantha ventures to two more major expositions, the Chicago World's Fair of 1893 (Columbian Exposition) and the St. Louis Exposition of 1904, cataloging their attractions as she had the marvels of the 1876 Centennial in "Filadelfy." She goes global with journeys to Europe and around the world, as always comparing the observed sights and cultures to life in Jonesville. Then, four decades after the publication of *My Opinions and Betsey Bobbet's*, a seasoned Samantha ends where she began—"eppisodin'" for suffrage and women's equal rights in *Samantha on the Woman Question* (1913).

The Expositions

In Holley's second book, *Josiah Allen's Wife as a P. A. and P. I.: Samantha at the Centennial* (1877), she had first used the occasion of a grand exposition as the backdrop for her social commentary on women's rights, fashion, temperance, race, and even capital punishment, white-collar crime, and war.[1] As usual, it took over half the book for Samantha, a representative of Jonesville as Promiscuous Advisor (P. A.) and Private Investigator (P. I.), to arrive in Philadelphia "to celebrate old Epluribus's birthday." Once there, Samantha described in detail exhibits housed in various buildings on the grounds. Along the way, she happens upon President Ulysses S. Grant and advises him on political rottenness, the great cause of Wimmen's Rights, and America's dishonest treatment of the Indians, among other matters.

The Woman's Pavilion and the range of contributions therein are chronicled with pride and "lofty feelin's." When she encounters a radical feminist who refuses to look at any buildings connected with men (whom she calls "mean snipes") and suggests taking a hammer to them to claim the vote, Samantha counsels patience and cooperation rather than vituperative confrontation. "I'd love to convince men of the truth, but it haint no use to take a hammer and try to knock unwelcome truths into anybody's head, male or female" (531). She underscores her "megum" tactic by using analogy and metaphor. "Nobody can git any water by breakin' up a chunk of ice with a axe; not a drop; you have got to thaw it out gradual; jest like men's and wimmen's prejudices in the cause of Wimmen's Rights. Public sentiment is the warm fire that is a goin' to melt this cold hard ice of injustice that we are contendin' ag'inst; laws haint good for much if public opinion don't stand behind 'em pushin' 'em onward to victory" (531). Given that it was 72 years after the Seneca Falls Convention and 43 years after *Samantha at the Centennial* before the suffrage amendment was finally passed, Samantha's use of the seed metaphor is particularly apt.

> . . . jest like all patient toilers for the Right, [Nature] plants the seed, and then lets it take time to swell out, and git full to bustin' with its own convictions and desires to grow, till it gits so sick of the dark ground where it is hid, and longs so for the light and the free air above it, that it can't be kep' back a minute longer, but soars right up of its own free will and accord, towards the high heavens and the blessed sunlight. But if seeds haint good for nothin', they wont come up; all the sunshine and rain on earth can't make 'em grow, nor cultivators, nor horse rakes, nor nothin'.
> And so with principles. (532)

As she would do again in *Samantha at the World's Fair*, Samantha looks to Columbia as the female symbol of America. "Columbia has got her high heeled shoes on, as you may say, and is showin' off, tryin' to see what she can do. She has been keepin' house for a hundred years, and been a addin' to her house every year, and repairin' of it and gettin' housen stuff together, and now she is havin' a regular house warmin', to show off, what a housekeeper she is" (496).

Sixteen years after *Samantha at the Centennial*, Holley was asked to write about the Columbian Exposition in Chicago. Her popularity allowed her to ask for and receive $14,000 for the book. In turn, the publishers sold a first edition run of 76,000 copies and subsequently reprinted 12 editions.[2] In the preface to *My Opinions* Josiah had whined about who would read it when it was "rote." In the preface to *Samantha at the World's Fair*, the last book to use this mode of entrance to the subject, Josiah now sees Samantha's popularity as a boon to his chances of elevation to salesman in the Jonesville Cheese Factory and claims an undeserved role in past achievements. He encourages her to write about the World's Fair, "like *we* wrote" for Filadelfy. *Our* reputation and popularity must be kept up. *We* can't afford to slight the fair and make everybody mad. Though "gaulded" by his pronouns and encumbered by the magnitude of the task, Samantha finally agrees: "Josiah, We will write the book."

Though she followed her usual custom of using guidebooks, maps, and other works as she had for *Samantha at the Centennial* and would for *Samantha at the St. Louis Exposition*, Holley did visit the Chicago World's Fair, albeit after she had written the book.

> I always detest a crowd, it always made me weary and half sick. And I told my publisher, Dr. Funk, afterwards that I could never have written the book had I visited the Fair first. So many scenes and people passing before me constantly weighed down my mind with the endless multitudes of things seen and heard, a bewildering riot of confusion and discordant noises.
>
> But at home in my quiet study with big maps of the Fair grounds and buildings, and lists of contents, I could in fancy happily walk down those beautiful paths and stand before those stately buildings with my faithful partner and in the happy quiet describe what I saw with my mental vision. Every immense crowd has the same general features, and one who has a Josiah for an escort finds plenty to write about.[3]

Given this writing strategy, Holley must have indulged a private giggle at the irony when she penned Samantha's rhapsody about on-site observation: "It would be jest as easy to comprehend the wonder of this

Exposition by readin' about it, as it would be for any one to try to judge Niagara by lookin' at a pan of dishwater" (237).

Once again in *Samantha at the World's Fair*, Holley offers predictable sentimental stories of the slum landlord whose daughter dies because of the squalor he ignored in the interest of profit, the small girl murdered by an intoxicated man, the eventual rewards to reunited lovers of constancy, duty to family, patience and sacrifice. Descriptions, often in eye-watering detail, of the fishery department, the horticulture exhibit, Machinery Hall, and so on, at the exposition do in fact read like a catalog. The writing seems as tired as Samantha's feet at the end of a long day on the fairgrounds. What energy there is in this narrative is summoned for Samantha's account of the Woman's Building and her continued commitment to equity for her "sect."

From the dedication ["To Columbia—who has jest sailed out and discovered woman. And to the sect discovered—This book is dedicated."] to the interpretation of statues to the Woman's Building, Samantha is unwavering in her eye for the role of gender.[4] In previous books, Holley had noted that in their depiction of abstract ideas public statues symbolically reflect the relative places of men and women in society. In *Sweet Cicely*, for example, Josiah had hurried home to recount the dispute that "had rosen" among the leading minds of Jonesville over the female "figger of liberty" being sculpted for the courthouse "cupelow." Josiah and his friends thought it should be "depictered" as a man—with whiskers, pantaloons, standing collar, and boots and spurs. Josiah was the one who insisted on the spurs. Samantha agrees that in these United States, Liberty was a man and to be consistent "ort" to be portrayed with "whiskers and overcoat and a standin' collar." To Josiah's insistence on spurs, Samantha presents an alternative:

> Instead of the spurs on his boots, he might be depictered as settin' his boot-heel onto the respectful petition of fifty thousand wimmen, who had ventured to ask him for a little mite of what he wus s'posed to have quantities of—Freedom.
>
> Or . . . he might be depictered as settin' on a judgment-seat, and wavin' off into prison an intelligent Christian woman,[5] who had spent her whole noble, useful life in studyin' the laws of our nation, for darin' to think she had as much right under our Constitution, as a low, totally ignorant coot who would most likely think the franchise wus some sort of a meat-stew.
>
> . . . That will give Liberty jest as imperious and showy a look as spurs would, and be fur more historick and symbolical. (*Cicely*, 133)

At the World's Fair the impressive statue of Columbia flanked by female "figgers" representing Science, Industry, Literature, and other disciplines, convinces Samantha that Columbia has indeed discovered woman at last and means to do right by her. A solid silver statue of a woman named Justice is likewise a sign of hope. Up to now, women had been treated much better "in stun" (stone) than in life. Surely, Samantha reasons, a nation wouldn't make a woman its symbol of Justice if it meant to continue denying her the rights of "the poorest dog that walks the globe."

As expected the first place Samantha wants to visit at the fair is the Woman's Building. Josiah agrees, assuming it wouldn't take long to see what women had brought. After all, it would be all tattin' and ornaments and flowers. Exhilarated by the sight of what her "sect" had achieved, Samantha describes in detail the range of women's contributions including building and interior design, woodcarvings, paintings, sculptures, books, inventions, model kindergarten, kitchen, and "horsepital," embroideries, tapestries, tattin', philanthropic societies, and international associations. Women had juried the exhibits as well, leading Samantha to call for the right to sit on juries when more is at stake. "It [Congress] has let wimmen tell which is the best piece of woosted work, or tattin'; now let her be judged by her peers when life or death is the award meted out to 'em" (258).

Samantha at the St. Louis Exposition (1904) offers little that is new in the Samantha/Josiah lexicon of travel and discussion. Samantha is again a tour guide, taking advantage of the fairground setting to relish the wonders of modern times (electricity, telephone, wireless telegraph, and grammophone) and decry the persistence of the liquor interests, political scandals, war, racism, and injustice to women.

At the Centennial Exposition the Woman's Pavilion had been almost a "sideshow," mounted by dedicated citizens without government support. The Woman's Building at the Chicago World's Fair was officially sanctioned and supported, a showpiece for women's achievements and contributions to the cultures of the world. Taking advantage of this popular shared cultural exhibit, Holley uses it to laud advances and lament continued inequities. By the time Samantha visits the St. Louis Exposition honoring the centennial of the Louisiana Purchase, she proudly points to what she perceives to be progress made toward the goal of shared humanity of men and women. Near the end of the narrative, she praises the good management of the Hall of Lady Managers:

In this Exposition there is no separate place fenced off for wimmen's exhibit. They carry the idee here that good work is equally valuable when done by man or woman. They claim that works of art, invention, manufacture, etc., are as sexless as religion. . . .
I wuz glad enough to see it, it seems to bring us nigher to the day of justice and true liberty for all. That glorious day hain't dawned yet (wimmen are still classed in law with idiots, criminals and lunaticks). But by standin' on tip-toe I can catch a faint glow in the East showin' that the day is goin' to break in rosy splendor bime-by. (*St. Louis Exposition,* 300–301)

In a rare exception to the usual home-and-hearth scene that closes Holley's books, Samantha and Josiah are not back in Jonesville, though they are leaving for home the next day. The final image is one of fireworks illuminating the night sky over the fair, perhaps signaling enlightenment for the young century.

The Globetrotting Granny

Holley's editors wanted to send her to Europe and then around the world in preparation to write Samantha's observations. She declined the trips but wrote the books. The *Boston Times* declared *Samantha in Europe* (1895) the best travel book since Twain's *The Innocents Abroad*.[6] *Around the World with Josiah Allen's Wife,* serialized in 1899 and published in book form in 1905, found Samantha in even more exotic places less familiar to the increasingly mobile American traveler. Samantha's direct experience with other cultures provides a forum for comparison to U.S. culture. In *Samantha in Europe* her encounters both in America and abroad with Al Faizi, an inquisitive missionary to the United States from some unspecified country in the East, serve to expose the differences between the American ideal and reality, as seen through the eyes of an outsider.

There is little moralizing about women's rights and temperance in *Samantha in Europe.* Instead, Samantha demonstrates "her conviction that the serious business of government and industry needs to be humanized, regardless of national or international politics. She concludes that one place is not better or worse than another, only different."[7] Cousin Martin Smith, a wealthy Gilded Age industrialist with no conscience, invites Samantha and Josiah to accompany him and his children on a European tour. It turns out that his motive for the trip is simply that he feels an exhaustive study is expected of anyone who lays any claim to fashion. To that end, he devotes as much as one week to each nation. Martin rushes them from country to country, always chauvinistic in putting America ahead of all others. He is arrogant, patronizing, and greedy in his business dealings, preferring the efficiency and profit of running his trolley cars on a swift schedule with no fenders to the expenditure of any money to guard life and limb. Predictably, the tale ends back home with the death of Martin's young son, who dies under the wheels of his father's unguarded trolley wheels. Martin repents, vowing to work for the poor as his son had wanted to do.

In *Around the World* Holley creates an alternative to the avaricious monopolist in Robert Strong, an industrialist who feels he only holds his wealth and "big manufactory" in trust. This time the trip is a healing voyage Samantha undertakes because her grandson Tommy needs to recuperate from a lung ailment and measles that have dangerously weakened him. The traveling group includes Robert Strong, three other women, and eventually Josiah when he catches up to them just before they sail.

Descriptions of sights, language, foods, and customs alternate with sermons/conversations of temperance, gentility, treatment of women, gambling, boxing as brutish recreation, colonialism, war, and capitalism. Arvilly, the book agent, peddles her tome on the twin American idols, Intemperance and Greed, and preaches the more radical line. Miss Meechim, the genteel "maiden lady by choice," chaperones Dorothy and cautions against the terrible state of matrimony. Samantha, of course, takes the moderate approach and continues to "walk all the way around a topic before makin' pronouncements about it."

With Robert Strong and his City of Justice, Holley creates a socialist utopia where owners and workers are partners laboring toward the same goal.

> He says he don't want to coin a big fortune out of other men's sweat and brains. He wants to march on with the great army of toilers, and not be carried ahead of it on a down bed. He says he wants to feel that he is wronging no man by amassing wealth out of the half-paid labor of their best years, and that he is satisfied with an equal and reasonable share of the labor and capital invested. He has the best of men in his employ and they are all well paid and industrious; all well-to-do, able to live well, educate their children well, and have time for some culture and recreation for themselves and their families. (21)

Samantha lambasts the monopoly as "the great American brigand hid in the black forest of politics. It has seized Labor in its clutches and wrings a ransom out of every toiler in the land" (382). She praises the profit-sharing that gives workers a stake in Strong's success. In the City of Justice, the owner mingles with the workers, intemperance is not allowed, and the physical work environment is safe and congenial. Miss Meechim finds it more genteel for the owner and his family to be distanced from the poor. Holley sees that the cost of gentility is inhumane treatment of the poor for the elevation and separation of the rich. As in previous works, in *Around the World* the arrogant rich[8] who ignore common decency and shared humanity always receive their comeuppance, whether through violence, accident, or disease.

When Holley turns to issues of colonialism, imperialism, or war, she uses the folksy analogy. In *Samantha at the Centennial* Samantha had referred to England's colonial empire as "the farm left to [Widder Albert] by her uncle George." The inhabitants "work her farm on shares" (514). In *Around the World* she sympathizes with the situation of Queen Liliukolani of the Sandwich Islands on the loss of her throne and property. "Why, how should any of us feel to have a neighbor walk in when we wuz havin' a family quarrel and jest clean us out of everything—kitchen stove, bureau, bed and beddin' and everything; why, it would rile us to our depths, any on us" (112). In fact, it reminded her of the time their neighbor Bill Yerden appropriated their woodsy island and fenced it in with "bob" wire while Josiah was sick. Queen Liliukolani advises Samantha that if she is ever a queen, "don't let any other nation protect you. Protectin' . . . has been the ruin of more than one individual and nation" (114).

In earlier works Holley had argued against the age of consent statutes and the practice of selling young girls into prostitution (called the white slave trade).[9] In *Around the World* Samantha tells the tale of a very young girl they meet on the trip who is tempted by entertainment, made senseless by intoxicating spirits, and sold and used by grown men. She dies in degradation and despair. Again, in her last book, Holley attacks the "criminal inconsistency" of the barbarous laws men have made when Josiah trivializes Samantha's ideas:

> Sez she, "A girl must be twenty-one when she is considered by men lawmakers wise enough to sell them a hen, or buy a cat. But yet at the age of ten in one state, twelve in another, she is considered by them wise and prudent enough to sell them the crowning jewel of her life with the pay-

ment of lifelong shame, agony, and despair, and mebby a little candy. Men make such laws," sez she, "not for their own sweet young girls, but for some other men's daughters, just like the infamous White Slave traffic that sells every year thousands and thousands of young girls into a livin' death." (*Josiah Allen on the Woman Question*, 65)

At the close of both *Europe* and *Around the World* the globe-trotting grandparents have seen the sights, moralized on the social issues, compared the world to their little corner in Jonesville, and gladly returned to home and family.

Potpourri

Three more books would be published between *Around the World* and *Samantha on the Woman Question*, none of which carries the humorous energies of earlier works. *Samantha vs. Josiah, Being the Story of a Borrowed Automobile and What Came of It* (1906) referred to in the chapter on gentility, is primarily an exploration of the natural and supernatural. Through Samantha, Holley recounts stories of the psychic and occult she had collected over the years, many of which had happened to her friends and would also appear in her autobiography. Laid up because of an injury sustained while trying to be foolishly fashionable in an automobile, Josiah is a captive audience for Samantha's illustrations of spiritual phenomenon. The skeptical Josiah always promotes some reasonable explanation for the phenomenon while Samantha is convinced of the presence of otherworldly spirits acting in the material world. With the exception of "The Male Magdalene," cited earlier, the bulk of this narrative is repetitious and dull.

In 1909 *Samantha on Children's Rights* was published. Throughout her work, Holley had championed children, whose mothers need the vote in order to protect them from draconian labor conditions in urban factories, age of consent laws, and so forth. In her own life, she had periodically taken in young boys who needed help and had informally adopted May Shaver, who by 1909 was married and a mother herself.[10] Samantha has been a doting stepmother and grandmother who recognized the frailties and relished the virtues of Tirzah Ann and Thomas Jefferson. In *Samantha on Children's Rights*, she tells of yet another mother interested only in being fashionable who leaves her children to the care of nurses and servants. She depicts a woman poet who rhapsodizes about home and children in her poetry but is raising ill-disciplined, raggedy, sassy children. Samantha advises her to make her own children works of art and try to care for them. Holley's view is clearly that mothers should tend their own children.[11]

Samantha even describes what would now be called fetal-alcohol syndrome. A woman who wears tight corsets throughout her pregnancy and drinks large quantities of stimulants at the direction of her fashionable but wrong-headed doctor gives birth to "an idiot." This time a mother's aspirations to gentility have endangered not only her own good health but that of her unborn child. Would that she had ridden a bicycle instead. Samantha advises another young woman to ignore her fiancé's objections that riding was unladylike and unwomanly. She hits on all cylinders of the cultural arguments regarding femininity, propriety, and physical capacities encapsulated in the bicycle craze of the 1880s and 1890s when she claims that "riding the wheel" is health-restoring exercise and demands sensible short skirts for safety.[12]

The main theme with regard to children's rights boils down to parents setting the proper example by their actions. "But as long as you do the same thing yourself [as mother has told child not to do], and teach Jack to do it, in the most powerful way, the way of example, you hadn't ort to whip him. For that is one theme for which I have labored long and feel deeply, to not blame children for what we do ourselves and teach them to do" (144).

The tale ends with the hackneyed story of ever-constant lovers finally free to marry, the death of young Jack who sacrifices his life to save another child, and the reformation of parents who are finally moved by tragedy to follow Samantha's parental advice.

Samantha at Coney Island and a Thousand Other Islands (1911) exposes foolish fashion and reunites faithful lovers true to one another during a 20-year separation. Samantha looks with pride on the Thousand Islands, which were located in her North Country, and allows that the fire destroying downstate Coney Island was not altogether regrettable. It's another chance for Samantha to offer travel observations—nothing new, nothing very funny.

Final Words: Woman Question Redux

Marietta Holley ends where she had begun. Forty years after *My Opinions and Betsey Bobbet's*, her last two prose works again center on "wimmen's rites." *Samantha on the Woman Question* (1913) is the first book in which Holley's name supplanted Josiah Allen's Wife as author. In most ways

Samantha on the Woman Question is a belaboring of ideas Samantha has preached since the beginning. In fact, entire sections from Holley's 1885 temperance novel *Sweet Cicely* are lifted from the earlier work and deposited in the latter. Samantha's trip to Washington, D.C., to tackle government officials is rendered nearly word for word, except that the sufferings of the Dorlesky Burpy family are now the agonies of the Serepta Pester clan. Holley's self-plagiarism seems to suggest a weariness and a heaviness of heart and spirit: after all these years what more can I say and why should I still be needing to say it.

Nevertheless, though most of the book is redundant, Holley does celebrate progress where it has been made and exploits current events for her reformist purposes. As she had done in the past, Samantha takes aim at women who stand in the way of women's rights. This time the foil is her relative Lorinda, who bristles at Samantha's unwomanly conduct and goals. In lines that could have been written to describe Phyllis Schlafly during the Equal Rights Amendment debate of the 1980s, Samantha plays on the term "anti-suffragist" (or "antis") and skewers the seeming hypocrisy of women she calls "She Auntys." ". . . old Miss Vincent . . . wuz a ardent She Aunty and very prominent in the public meetin's the She Auntys have to try to compel the Suffragists not to have public meetin's. They talk a good deal in public how onwomanly and immodest it is for wimmen to talk in public. And she wuz one of the foremost ones in tryin' to git up a school to teach wimmen civics, to prove that they mustn't ever have anything to do with civics" (62–63).

Over the years, some laws had indeed changed and by 1913 limited or full suffrage had been granted in about one-fourth of the states. In reply to Samantha's litany of lawful inequities suffered by the Pesters, Lorinda claims that women's voting would have no effect on such matters as equal pay. Her "poor relation" Euphrasia Pottle begs to differ. One of her daughters works in a factory and receives about one-half what a man earns for the same work; another teaches in the public school and doesn't earn even half as much as male teachers and endures "onhealthy," crowded conditions. Her niece's experience, however, is considerably different: "Ellen teaches in a state where wimmen vote and she gits the same wages men git for the same work, and her school rooms are bright and pleasant and sanitary, and the pupils, of course, are well and happy. And if you don't think wimmen can help in such public matters just go to Seattle and see how quick a bad man wuz yanked out of his public office and a good man put in his place, mostly by wimmen's efforts and votes" (51–52).

To Lorinda's assertion that suffrage would make women neglect their homes and children, Samantha counters that "wherever wimmen has voted they have looked out first of all for the children's welfare. They have raised the age of consent, have closed saloons and other places of licensed evil, and in every way it has been their first care to help 'em to safer and more moral surroundin's . . ." (53).

In *Samantha on the Woman Question* Holley takes advantage of mass rallies that would be familiar to the reader and recognizes the international nature of the suffrage struggle. Philander Daggett, president of the Jonesville Creation Searchin' Society and confirmed "He Aunty," thought the Searchers should go to the New York City suffrage parade to help the "She Auntys" sneer at the marchers. Samantha, of course, views the splendor of that Woman's Parade, describing the range of participants including physicians, lawyers, nurses, authors, journalists, artists, social workers, shop girls, dressmakers, milliners, clerks, and college girls.

In the final scenes, Samantha describes the Creation Searchin' Society's "indignation meetin'," a piece that includes references both to the march on Washington, D.C., the day before Woodrow Wilson's inauguration and to the "doin's of the militant Suffragettes" in England.[13] The Searchers have gathered to be indignant about the "turrible doin's" across the Atlantic Ocean and to come up with concrete suggestions for their British brethren before this infection spreads to the angels of their very own homes. In an example of the occasional, original gem salted in the recycled terrain of Holley's later works, Samantha recounts the meeting from her secret vantage point in the balcony behind the melodeon. Searchers' suggestions for controlling women who ask for their rights range from killing them off to giving them a dose of something sickening to muzzling them. Each suggestion carries an objection: it would have a disastrous effect on the world's populations; a dose of wormwood would interfere with their other rights, like cooking, cleaning, taking care of the children; you can't keep a woman from talkin' without endangering her very life. For his part, Josiah says that nothing short of a Gatlin gun could keep Samantha from saying what was on her mind, and he didn't want her sick and incapacitated so she couldn't cook for him.

After much debate, the only thing they can come up with is a resolution of sympathy for their British brethren. When she sees Josiah so dejected at their failure and about to "bust out weeping" in front of the Searchers, she forgets herself and calls out from her hiding place: "Here is sunthin' that no one has seemed to think on at home or abroad. How would it work to stop the trouble by givin' the wimmen the rights they ask for, the rights of any other citizen?" Because the Searchers know that no women are allowed in the Society, some of them thought the voice had come from another "spear." So some are running away from ghosts, others are searching for women spies, and Samantha meanwhile "scooted acrost lots and wuz to home a-knittin before the men got there." In keeping with her constant "megum" stance, Samantha does not condone the violent tactics of the English Suffragettes, but she wholeheartedly believes in the justice of their cause.

Ironically, it is Josiah who pens Holley's final published words in *Josiah Allen on the Woman Question* (1914).[14] Deeply wounded for years by Samantha's "writin' agin the righteous cause of man's superiority to wimmen," Josiah had nevertheless postponed writing his own book until now because he anticipated that her weak woman's mind would get "ruffled up" and ruin her cooking. Because women are rising up on every side claiming to be equal to men, he fears he may have waited too long. When Josiah asks Samantha what she thinks of his project to destroy female suffrage, she hardly quails at the prospect: "When I wuz a girl we had a Debatin' School, and there wuz one feller that we always tried to git on the side opposite to us, his talk and arguments wuz such a help to us. I hain't no objections to your writing the book, Josiah" (15). As Kate Winter notes: "Not surprisingly, the arguments are Josiah's, but the voice is Samantha's. As if her patience had run out, Samantha is letting Josiah run on in his absurdities, assuming that any right-minded person in the twentieth century would recognize his foolishness."[15]

Josiah Allen on the Woman Question offers the same well-worn arguments but also affords the opportunity to indulge the utopian vision of egalitarian marriage as lived by Sime Bentley's nephew out in Illinois, a state that had enfranchised women in 1913. Regardless of Josiah's objections, a new day was dawning. Holley published in each of five decades and championed the cause of women's rights and temperance in nearly every book. At the end of the run with *Josiah Allen on the Woman Question*, it would still be another six years before passage of the Nineteenth Amendment to the Constitution in 1920, ensuring the franchise for all women citizens. Samantha had always said that you can't "sow your seeds and pick your posies the same day." Holley lived to see passage of both suffrage and prohibition.[16] Fortunately, she lived a long life.

Chapter Six

Writ Down by Males, and Translated by 'Em Mostly

By the time she died in 1926, Marietta Holley's works were largely unread and out of print, her popularity long before eclipsed by a more urbane, sophisticated brand of humor and her causes more clearly identified with the nineteenth century. In the canon of American literature and humor, the author whose nom de plume had been a household word for decades and whose books had transformed the genre of American vernacular humor to advocate a feminist reordering of cultural values was relegated to footnotes or ignored altogether. This last chapter will discuss the performance history surrounding the Holley literary personae, address the course of Holley's literary reputation, and summarize her considerable contributions as author, social critic, and funny foremother.

Samantha on Stage

The performance history associated with Holley's characters is something of a drama itself, one that illustrates the reach of her popularity among the general public then and now, the manipulation of a feminist sensibility for antifeminist ends, and the revival of a foremother for a new generation.

The success of *My Opinions and Betsey Bobbet's* gave rise immediately to various three-dimensional incarnations of the main characters in informal gatherings as well as amateur and professional performance venues around the country. In "How I Wrote My First Books," Holley mentions a club formed in Chicago, "called the Betsy Bobbet Club, each member taking a character and name from the book, and sending a report of their meetings to the author. Josiah Allen, president of the club, personated by a dignified Chicago businessman, came to Pierrepont Manor to see the author, who he said was giving them so much pleasure . . ." (405). One club in Chicago included a senator and three Presbyterian clergymen. Clara Barton occasionally joined in, preferring to read the part of Betsey. By spring 1880, Betsey Bobbet Clubs were performing

81

dramatic readings all across New York State, using local talent interpreting well-known episodes from the Samantha books. Several vocal ensembles even became known as the "Jonesville Choir" and gave concerts in the Cooper Opera House in Adams and elsewhere.[1]

It seems curious, at the very least, that admirers would name their clubs after the sentimental Betsey Bobbet character and choose the foolish Josiah Allen as their leader. Although Holley did not remark on that particular irony, she did voice her opinion on the various interpreters over the years of her "thought-children."

> Many elocutionists have personated Samantha, or endeavored to do so, but few have succeeded, nearly all of them making her too tragic, too bizarre, she being a combination of earnestness, common sense, and calmness; in fact, it was and is her constant endeavor to be megum herself, and influence her excitable partner to be so. But many of these elocutionists are far from megumness, being inclined to tear emotion into tatter's, and they make Samantha's common-sense sayings and eloquent eppisodin's seem like the ravings of hysteria." ("How I Wrote," 405)

While visiting Saratoga Springs, Holley attended a reception at which the well-known elocutionist Anna Randell Deihl had been invited to give a reading. In her autobiography, Holley recounted her displeasure with Deihl's interpretation. "Mrs. Deihl's interpretation of Samantha's character was like many others. From her rendering of Samantha's common sense words one would picture her as a violent termagant, instead of the quiet philosopher she always intended to be, looking on at the show of life passing before her and gravely commenting on its fashions and its follys, as well as its nobler aspects" (Ch. 10).

Perhaps the most ironic twist in the contemporaneous performance history, particularly considering Holley's focus on women's rights, was that men, too, impersonated Samantha. One such performer met with her fond approval, another with bitter disdain at his betrayal and greed. Of Bostonian S. Homer Eaton, whom she heard read in New York, Holley said:

> He dressed the part to perfection with a white cap over his hair combed smoothly around his face, a big white apron and a collar fastened by an enormous cameo pin. He told me that when he was impersonating her, he entirely lost sight of his own individuality, and was for the time really Samantha Allen.———I could not ask for any change in his dress or manner of reciting. I think his subject that evening was Samantha's talk

about bringing up Tirzah and Thomas Jefferson, and as he finished he came directly to me, holding out his hand and asking me with his voice and his eyes if I liked it, and I said to him, and certainly meant it, "It is perfect!"[2]

The most famous male impersonator of Samantha was professional actor Neil Burgess, who also wrote and performed a play called "The Widow and the Elder," based on Frances Whitcher's Widow Bedott character. In "The County Fair," cowritten with Charles Barnard, Burgess played the sharp-tongued old maid, Miss Abigail Prue. Both plays enjoyed popular success and extended production runs throughout the 1880s. Burgess wrote to Holley informing her that he intended to start on the road with a play called *Betsey Bobbet*. At the behest of her lawyer, Burgess was summoned to Adams for a meeting with Holley regarding her copyright to the names of her characters. He agreed to pay a weekly royalty for permission to use the names of Holley's characters and for plot material he was to adapt into his dramatic version. In addition, Holley insisted that there should be nothing "coarse or off color" in his adaptation.[3]

Initially, all went well. Holley attended the successful premiere in Providence, Rhode Island, approved of the interpretation, received the royalties, and felt confident that the "iron-clad" contract was being honored. "But the net must indeed be a strong one that would hold a theatrical star."[4] In 1878 Burgess moved the play to New York City, changed the name of the play to *Vim, or a Visit to the Puffy Farm*, renamed the characters, transformed the figure of Samantha from dignified, homespun philosopher to grotesque, sensational termagent, and discontinued royalty payments. Samantha was henceforth dubbed Tryphena Puffy, and no program or review even mentions Marietta Holley. This successful version ran for 200 performances at the Bijou Theater in 1883 and was revived periodically until 1888 in New York and Boston.[5]

The large, robust Burgess created and then impersonated female characters with the apparent intention of ridiculing women. In her analysis of the script for *Vim*, Linda Morris suggests that "not only is Burgess's Tryphena Puffy a shrew, she is a stereotype of a shrew. . . . Certainly we are not meant to admire such a woman, nor does she elicit our sympathy; nor can we imagine Neil Burgess feeling anything but smug contempt for Tryphena. Her shrewishness is totally uncalled for but is the most distinctive part of her personality; therein resides a good portion of the humor of *Vim*."[6] In fact, according to Morris, one of the central themes of *Vim* is "debunking the women's rights movement and the women who participated in it" (268).

Despite her feelings of shock and betrayal when she saw a performance of *Vim*, Holley followed her legal counsel's advice that it would be a waste of time and money to contest Burgess's violation of their contract. Meanwhile, *Betsey Bobbet: A Drama*, Holley's play published in 1880 that had evolved from the more informal presentations initiated by avid readers, was first presented by 30 young women at Clavarack College on the banks of the Hudson River in February 1881. It was still being revived in amateur productions, often for a charitable cause, by troupes in small cities and villages as far away as Ohio and Iowa into the twentieth century. The Burgess burlesque, as insulting and misogynist as it was, apparently did not damage the continuing appeal of Holley's wise rustic. In fact, as late as 1916, the 80-year-old Holley negotiated with an unnamed movie company in Los Angeles interested in putting Samantha, Josiah, and Betsey on film in an adaptation of *Betsey Bobbet: A Drama*. Neither this nor one previous venture into the medium of film bore fruit, and she concluded that writing for the movies was a "sheer waste of time and energy."[7]

So, it is thoroughly in keeping with both the written dramatic monologue form and previous efforts to give voice to Holley's characters that more than 100 years later the persona of Samantha once again has returned to the stage. This time she "episodes" in a one-woman show called *Samantha "Rastles" the Woman Question*, based on the Holley books and written and performed by Jane Curry.

I think it's more than a little "dubersome" to speak of oneself in the third person. So I'll exercise my prerogative as a recovering academic to speak plainly. In the tradition of Hal Holbrook impersonating Mark Twain, I have traveled nationally and internationally since 1982 introducing Holley's work to thousands of audience members. My portrayal features Samantha's common-sense feminism and highlights historical struggles for women's rights that resonate with still-current issues and images of gender discourse. I've performed as Samantha in Grange halls, libraries, hotel banquet rooms, church sanctuaries, school auditoriums, Chautauqua tents, on major stages, and even at an Israeli kibbutz. I've performed for groups ranging from conferences of feminist scholars to workers at the Naval Surface Warfare Center, from extension homemakers groups to the Plumbing, Heating, and Cooling Contractors of Minnesota.

What I can say from over a decade's experience at playing the Samantha character is that modern audiences of men and women are engaged and delight-

ed by her humor, her anecdotal accounts of conversations with foils, her witty way of illuminating illogic and injustice. People who might be put off by the cacography of the written word have no trouble at all understanding the spoken dialect language that carries Samantha's ideas. Their eyes twinkle, they chortle, they guffaw. Sometimes they laugh until tears run down their cheeks; sometimes they even weep at the familiarity of Samantha's experiences. Between long-married "pardners," I see the occasional gentle elbow to the ribs and knowing nods when Samantha's wit obviously hits home in their particular domestic situation. After many a show, a patron has approached me with a smile on her face and pain in her eyes, announcing that her husband is, alas, a lot like "Josiah." Typically, they remark that we've come a long way but still have a goodly distance to travel.

Perhaps my favorite comment came after a show sponsored by a local historical society in northern Minnesota. A crusty, retired trapper from the area announced while buying his ticket that he'd seen the picture in the paper and wanted to come to a program about women who were old-fashioned, the way they were supposed to be. After the show, he was asked how he had liked it. His laconic response is music to an educator's ear: "Kinda sorry I came to this. Might have to change some of my idees."

In their *1978 anthology,* America's Humor: From Poor Richard to Doonesbury, *Walter Blair and Hamlin Hill devoted only two pages to women's humor. In a paragraph that confuses author and her persona, they wrote of Holley: "In the era of the Phunny Phellows, Marietta Holley edged closer to today's women comic writers when she created and quoted a Phunny Phemale, 'Josiah Allen's Wife,' Samantha. Ms. Holley, a feminist, satirized religious hypocrisy, political skulduggery, and male chauvinism. But she was an unschooled rustic with sound mare sense, a Christian, a loving wife and a model housekeeper, and therefore could never have become as popular today as she did during her lifetime."*[8]

I continue to wonder which of the named characteristics would automatically disqualify her. Time and time again audiences prove Blair and Hill wrong.[9] *Holley said of reaction to her creations: ". . . everywhere I have ever been—East, West, North, or South—some one has said we have a perfect Josiah or Samantha living near us, or a Betsy Bobbett, . . . from which I am encouraged to think there must be a good deal of our common human nature in the characters."*[10] *Likewise, everywhere I travel, from Walla Walla to Tel Aviv, people say that Samantha reminds them of a favorite grandmother, a great-aunt, one spunky foremother or another who is recalled to them through Samantha's wit and wisdom.*

The Rise and Fall and Rise of Reputation

As discussed in the introduction, Holley's Josiah Allen's Wife was a "family friend from Mexico to Alaska," her "eppisodin's" assumed to have entertained as wide an audience as Mark Twain. Holley was a famous literary figure who might have become part of the Hartford literati had it not been for her shyness and timid nature. Never as self-effacing as her creator, Samantha alluded to her own fame on several occasions. When Samantha stood in the library of the Woman's Building at the Chicago World's Fair surprised at the sight of her own books "a-standin' up jest as noble and pert as if they wuz to home in the what-not behind the parlor door," she proudly assessed her impact as an author. ". . . I spoze the nation collected 'em together and sot 'em up there because it sets such a store by me. It is dretful fond of me, the nation is, and well it may be. I have stood up for it time and agin, and then I've done a sight for it in the way of advisin' and bracin' it up."[11] She wonders whether her books have done any good in the world. She "wanted 'em to like a dog" but sometimes felt "dubersome" about whether they had. Then, Samantha sidesteps boastfulness and pulls the rug out from under conceit:

> But I knew they had gin great enjoyment, I'd hearn on't. Why, the minister up to Zoar had told me of as many as seven relations of hisen, who, when they wuz run down and weak, and had kinder lost their minds, had jest clung to them books.
> In softenin' of the brain now, or bein' kicked on the head, or natural brain weakness—why, them books are invaluable, so I spoze. (241–42)

References to Holley's characters turn up in the writings of others from Wyoming to Canada. For example, Elinor Pruitt Stewart, whose *Letters of a Woman Homesteader* was the basis for the movie *Heartland*, twice refers to them in letters dated from April 1900, to November 1913. Speaking of a trip to the county seat with a neighbor, she says: "I had more fun to the square inch than Mark Twain or Samantha Allen *ever* provoked." In another letter she remarks: "As soon as I could, I made myself scarce about the granary and very busy about the house, and like Josiah Allen, I was in a very 'happified' state of mind." In *Anne of the Island* (circa 1910), one of the Anne of Green Gables series written by L. M. Montgomery from Prince Edward Island, Anne's college chum announces, "*My* mission is, as Josiah Allen says, 'to charm and allure.'"

As would be expected, critics both praised and dismissed Holley's efforts. The entry in the *National Cyclopaedia of American Biography*, written while Holley was still publishing her books, praises: "'Josiah Allen's Wife' . . . has written some of the most mirth-provoking books that have ever been given to the public, and her books have found a warm welcome with all classes, and are read in nearly every civilized country of the globe, having been translated into a number of languages. From Africa and Japan have come messages of warm appreciation, and the foreign press has been quite as appreciative as the American."[12]

In a piece written a few years before his death in 1937, Ellis Parker Butler located her popularity in the serious messages underlying Holley's humor: "Literally hundreds of thousands enjoyed her writings who could see nothing funny in Bill Nye, or any of the other professional humorists, not even Mark Twain. Hundreds of thousands took her to their hearts because they felt she was basing her humor soundly on a belief in temperance, woman's rights and the homely virtues, while other humorists were merely trying to be funny."[13]

In a review of Holley's second book, *Josiah Allen's Wife as a P. A. and P. I.: Samantha at the Centennial*, Samuel Clemens offered a bit of a backhanded compliment when he declared the work "brilliant, a grand improvement on the first."[14]

In her critical essay, "Attention and Neglect: The Reputations of Marietta Holley and Mark Twain," Charlotte Templin cites several contemporary reviews of Holley's work that "suggest a fair amount of condescension from the literary elite."[15] One of the most positive was found in a newspaper review from 1885 that refers to "the infinite variety of her wit and genius." One review of *Sweet Cicely* finds "good and genuinely humorous points" but predicts that Holley's kind of humor is "not destined to be immortal." Another finds the novel "wearisome" and "at least a hundred pages too long." The latter reviewer is not moved by the feminist arguments ("she raves about women's rights") but points approvingly to her views on "public affairs, e.g. her comments on the copyright law."

Several citations from the early twentieth century may skew the sample because Holley's best work was admittedly far behind her by then. One reviewer finds "genuine humor" in *Samantha vs. Josiah* but cautions that it should be read in small doses; another refers to Samantha's "weakly witty garrulity." In a review of *Samantha Among the Brethren* in 1891, the reviewer admires neither Holley's content or style: "No doubt the Cause of Eternal Justice gets very much the worst of it as does the cause of orthography. The two have always seemed to us to suffer together at the hands of humorists of the Marietta Holley sort. It is to be hoped that the humorists will be worsted in their turn and disappear . . . to the Limbo of vain things."[16]

Later critics, too, consigned Holley to a literary limbo. Whereas in *Horse Sense in American Humor* (1942), Walter Blair had devoted half a chapter to Holley and declared Samantha one of the most popular characters in American humor, as noted earlier, he and Hamlin Hill dismiss her in a paragraph in their 1978 anthology. In explaining his selections for a 1947 anthology of American humor, James Aswell says that Holley "most particularly . . . didn't amuse me." In a piece devoted to "Rural Humor of the Late Nineteenth Century," C. Carroll Hollis describes her work as "of interest to historians, not citizens."[17] Alfred Habegger called Holley "the most important wise old woman in nineteenth-century American literature" and "a pivotal figure in nineteenth-century female humor" whose books disappeared so rapidly because they were too preachy. He claimed that the "feminine" tradition of humor rested on the assumption of superiority and called Samantha a "populist superwoman" whose voice ultimately was unauthentic. His pronouncement is pretty close to "lighten up, Marietta." "'Populist' characters like . . . Samantha Allen have a vernacular power that finally seems a little factitious. They may speak as the natives speak, but something has been faked. They don't seem to feel the inner ease, the relaxed dignity that laughter requires. They don't take it easy."[18]

Literary reputation has often been seen as the result of a benign sorting out of quality, the literary canon as objectified as a bottle of milk in which the cream inevitably rises to the top. In her aforementioned essay, Charlotte Templin endorses a different view, one in which "literary reputation is a contingent phenomenon, the product of social and cultural forces."[19] Basically, literary reputations are made, not born. Writers relegated to the margins—especially men of color and women—have customarily challenged tenets of the dominant culture and offered alternative, often conflicting narratives about America and Americans. These writers, no matter how popular they might have been with the general public and/or a perceived constituency in their own time, have often been rendered invisible by elite cultural arbiters who don't share their experience or value their interpretations.

In assessing Holley's place in or absence from the canon of American literature, it is instructive to draw comparisons with Mark Twain. Holley and Twain were direct contemporaries who wrote in the vernacular tradition of the cracker-barrel philosopher. Some of their early works were issued by the same publisher, using the same illustrator and marketing them to the same public via subscription agents.[20] Both authors were famous as humorists, a literary category that lacked respect among academic canonizers. Both were critics of their culture. Both occasionally indulged in the very Victorian sentimental tradition they satirized. Both produced a large body of work uneven in quality.[21] As Templin points out, during her lifetime Holley enjoyed comparable standing with Twain, but she subsequently disappeared from the literary scene while Twain "came to be a figure through whom Americans were able to represent their culture to themselves and in that way to embody certain values that it was impossible for a woman to embody in a patriarchal culture."[22]

In noting the privileged status of the humorous writer to "mock the sacred" and reveal perceptions often at odds with official cultural rhetoric and practice, Nancy Walker, too, cites the different posthumous reputations of Holley and Twain: ". . . whereas Mark Twain's pointed satire on the evils of slavery in *Huck Finn* has been an enduring part of American literary and cultural history, Marietta Holley's equally pointed satire on opposition to female suffrage in *My Opinions and Betsey Bobbet's* has been, until recently, unavailable as a resource for understanding late-nineteenth-century attitudes and values."[23]

Given the low opinion of humorists generally, Templin suggests, even Twain's reputation had to undergo a metamorphosis in order for him to arrive as a Man of Letters. "This feat was accomplished by redescribing him as a moralist and philosopher, a keen observer of the world and a man with insight into human character." At that, his reputation was at a low point after his death and reservations were expressed about the quality of his work. Templin quotes critic Fred Louis Pattee's 1928 essay in which Pattee calls Twain a "thwarted creator": "He must go down in posterity as a collection of glorious fragments, as an enrichment to anthologies rather than as a maker of rounded masterpieces."[24]

Of course, Holley could also be described with these words. She was a moralist and philosopher, a keen observer whose insight into human character was refracted through the lens of women's experience. "Glorious fragments" abound in often wordy and repetitious longer works. Nevertheless, by the 1930s Twain's reputation was established, and *Huck Finn* declared to be his masterpiece. Holley was omitted from anthologies and generally forgotten.

Holley's gender, her feminism, her anachronistic comic style, and the low regard for humor as a literary vehicle combined to keep her light under a bushel. Her rejuvenation began in earnest in the 1970s and 1980s when primarily feminist scholars rediscovered her work and published articles in journals. They focused on Holley's women's rights and social reform themes, as well as her use of humor as a strategy to advocate reform to the general public. In the 1980s a biography was published as was an anthology of selections reprinted from Holley's narratives; her work was included in another anthology, *Redressing the Balance: American Women's Literary Humor from Colonial Times to the 1980s*. Finally, in 1990 a selection from one of Holley's novels was included in the *Heath Anthology of American Literature*, a milestone both because it represents "mainstream" recognition and because she and Twain are the only two nineteenth-century humorists included.[25]

Just as Holley's works both reflected and benefited from national reform movements of her day, renewed interest in reclaiming her for our literary and social history is no doubt at least partially due to the latter-day women's movement. Her humor resonates for many modern readers because a century later feminists are still sounding some of the same arguments Samantha tackled. In *The Feminization of American Culture*, Ann Douglas describes the process of researching and writing her book on nineteenth-century America. "I expected to find my fathers and my mothers; instead I discovered my fathers and my sisters. The best of the men had access to solutions, and occasionally inspiring ones, which I appropriate only with the anxiety and effort that attend genuine aspiration. The problems of the women correspond to mine with a frightening accuracy that seems to set us outside the process of history; the answers of even the finest of them were often mine, and sometimes largely unacceptable to me...."[26]

As an author, Marietta Holley used the conventions of an established vernacular humor tradition to undermine, not endorse, prevailing cultural values regarding gender spheres. A feminist innovator whose audience was probably mostly female, she transformed that tradition by offering an alternative to gentility in post–Civil War America. She dispatched familiar comic devices in the service of serious social reform that struck at the most basic assumptions of American culture. Whereas the comic reversal of opinionated, heavyset wife and henpecked, lightweight spouse had always been used to create sympathy for the beleaguered husband, Holley in effect "reverses the comic reversal."[27] Josiah is the smaller, dumber, prouder, and more irrational "pardner" who clumsily presents what can only be seen as the laughable logic of an inept man trying to preserve the power he undeservedly inherited by being born male. Hefty, loquacious Samantha is the strong, principled, authoritative, sage heroine.

Likewise, Holley used the travel format not as a metaphor of movement and unfettered freedom of the individual in a land of manifest destiny but as a means of observation into the workings of public spheres and confirmation of the values of community. Samantha is grounded in her home and village, attentive to its domestic and public rhythms, strengths, foibles, follies, and pretensions. Prose textured by a wealth of domestic detail provides unfailing comparison of everything "out there" to life in Jonesville.

It's true that Holley never subscribed to the notion that brevity is the soul of wit. And Samantha does get preachy and even sentimental and maudlin, anon or oftener. And Holley's later works are endlessly repetitious and sometimes read like the guidebooks she used in place of on-the-spot travel. However, to use a favorite Samantha aphorism: "Pick out the good and leave the bad is my theme in greens and politix." The good in Holley's work should claim for her an irrevocable place in a reformulated canon of American literary humor. Despite the anachronistic comic devices and historic distance, Samantha Smith Allen remains immediately accessible to contemporary sensibilities. Many of the issues Holley's literary persona articulated—equal pay, domestic abuse, affiliative status, women's role in the church, gendered language, children's rights, alcoholism, full representation in Congress, and more—continue to be front-page news in the popular media and topics of discussion among scholars, clergy, and civil servants. In fact, the only women's rights issue that is obviously outdated is female enfranchisement. And even then, during the 1980s when the Equal Rights Amendment was passed but fell short of ratification, the rhetoric surrounding that political debate—with promises of higher moral standards and warnings of unisex bathrooms—wasn't all that different from the extremes of both prosuffrage and antisuffrage arguments advanced and ridiculed by Samantha.

As a social critic, Holley used humor to disarm opponents, humanize the issues, and expose the disjunction between public ideology and private reality. As Samantha said: "You have to hold up the hammer of a personal incident to drive home the nail of Truth and have it clench and hold fast." As a humorist, Holley joined in attacks on the genteel culture and sentimental tradition but stood alone among her colleagues in the vernacular school by making the opponents rather than the advocates of women's rights the targets of social satire. As a funny foremother, the

Samantha persona is, as Ann Douglas surmised, more a sibling than a parent.

Marietta Holley was periodically called the "female Mark Twain." In their discussion following a funeral, Josiah became dejected and "dubersome," contemplating the eventual demise of his beloved. In an episode steeped in the concept of affiliative status and informed by observation of graveyards, Josiah proclaims his devotion by announcing what he had in mind for the inscription of Samantha's tombstone, if he could ever live through the grief of "rarin'" one up over her body. He had it laid out as follows, to wit: "Here lies Samantha, wife of Deacon Josiah Allen, Esquire, of Jonesville. Deacon in the Methodist Church, salesman in the Jonesville cheese factory, and a man beloved and respected by every one who knows him but to love him, and names him but to praise." She was, of course, "plumb" touched. Later, she allows that she has in mind to lay him out with a verse of poetry as well. To wit: "Here lies Josiah Allen, husband of Samantha Allen,———" She never gets to finish because an apoplectic Josiah protests that he would never be "drug down and demeaned" to the status of "husband of." Why, rather than to have that rared up over him, he'd just "ruther" not die at all![28]

As Samantha said of the wives of the Old Testament prophets, "folks ort to own up, male or female, and them old females ort to have justice done 'em." There is no need to claim that Mark Twain was the "male Marietta Holley." It is enough to claim her rightful place in the memorial gardens of our literary heritage. Next to the tombstone marking those who failed to give her her due—inscribed, to wit: "Often wrong. Never in doubt."

Samantha and Josiah as illustrated by Frederick Opper in Samantha at Saratoga, 1887.

Notes and References

Introduction

1. *The Critic* (January 1905): 6.
2. Kate Sanborn, *The Wit of Women* (New York: Funk & Wagnalls, 1885), 31.
3. Walter Blair, *Horse Sense in American Humor* (Chicago: University of Chicago Press, 1942), 231.
4. James D. Hart, ed., *The Oxford Companion to American Literature* (New York: Oxford University Press, 1941), 328.
5. *The National Cyclopedia of American Biography* (New York: James White, 1899), 278.
6. Frances Willard and Mary Livermore, *A Woman of the Century* (n.p.: n.p., 1893).
7. The performance history associated with Holley's works is discussed in chapter 6.
8. Marietta Holley, "How I Wrote My First Books," *Harper's Bazar* 45, no. 9 (September 1911): 405.
9. In addition to the books of Linda Morris, Nancy Walker, and Kate Winter, which will be cited extensively, other scholars and their work include: Shelley Armitage, "Marietta Holley: The Humorist as Propagandist," *Rocky Mountain Review*, 34, no. 4 (fall 1980): 193–201; Jane Curry, "Samantha 'Rastles' the Woman Question," *Journal of Popular Culture*, VIII, no. 4 (spring 1975): 805–24; Melody Graulich, "'Wimmen is my theme, and also Josiah': The Forgotten Humor of Marietta Holley," *The American Transcendental Quarterly*, no. 47–48 (summer/fall 1980): 187–98; Cheri Ross, "Nineteenth-Century Feminist Humor: Marietta Holley's 'Samantha Novels,'" *Journal of Midwest Modern Language Association*, 22, no. 2 (1989): 12–25; and "Transforming Fictional Genres: Five Nineteenth-Century American Feminist Novelists" (Ph.D. diss., Purdue University, 1991); Alice Sheppard, "From Kate Sanborn to Feminist Psychology: The Social Context of Women's Humor, 1885–1985," *Psychology of Women Quarterly* (1986): 155–70; Charlotte Templin, "Marietta Holley's Comic Critique of a Nineteenth-Century Ideology of Gender," *Thalia: Studies in Literary Humor*, 11, no. 2 (1990): 28–33, and "Attention and Neglect: The Reputations of Marietta Holley and Mark Twain," in manuscript; Emily Toth, "A Laughter of Their Own: Women's Humor in the United States," in William Bedford Clark and W. Craig Turner, eds., *Critical Essays on American Humor* (Boston: G. K. Hall, 1984); Nancy Walker, "Wit, Sentimentality and the Image of Women in the Nineteenth Century,"

American Studies, XXII, no. 2 (fall 1981): 5–22; Patricia Williams, "The Crackerbox Philosopher: The Novels of Marietta Holley," *American Humor: An Interdisciplinary Newsletter*, 7, no. 1 (1980), 16–21.

   10.   Among the more well-known pioneering critical accounts, Holley is given extensive treatment only in Walter Blair's *Horse Sense in American Humor*. She is a name among names in Jennette Tandy's *Crackerbox Philosophers* (1925); she rates only a footnote in Jesse Bier's *Rise and Fall of American Humor* (1968). And even though Samantha fits the description of what Constance Rourke called a "Yankee oracle," there is no reference to Holley in Rourke's classic *American Humor: A Study of the National Character* (New York: Doubleday, 1931). In fact, with the exception of Emily Dickinson, she overlooks women writers and claims: "Women had played no essential part in the long sequence of the comic spirit in America" (118).

   11.   Linda Morris, *Women Vernacular Humorists in Nineteenth-Century America: Ann Stephens, Frances Whitcher, and Marietta Holley* (New York: Garland Publishing, 1988), 1.

   12.   Walter Blair described *horse sense* as "the same thing as common sense, homespun philosophy, pawkiness, cracker-box philosophy, gumption, or mother-wit" and suggests the terms can be used interchangeably (*Horse Sense*, vi). For other discussions of the vernacular tradition, see Morris, *Women Vernacular Humorists*, ch. 1; Walter Blair, *Native American Humor* (San Francisco: Chandler Publishing, 1960); Franklin J. Meine, *Tall Tales of the Southwest; An Anthology of Southern and Southwestern Humor, 1830–1860* (New York: Alfred A. Knopf, 1930); as well as the Rourke and Tandy volumes cited in note 11.

   13.   Linda Morris, *Women's Humor in the Age of Gentility: The Life and Works of Frances Miriam Whitcher* (Syracuse, N.Y.: Syracuse University Press, 1992), 5–6.

   14.   Hennig Cohen and William B. Dillingham, eds., *Humor of the Old Southwest* (Boston: Houghton Mifflin, 1964), introduction. For a discussion of characteristics of the Down East, Literary Comedian, and Local Color categories, see Walter Blair, *Native American Humor* (Scranton, Pa.: Chandler Publishing, 1937). Besides Samuel Clemens and Seba Smith, these traditions included Johnson J. Hooper (Simon Suggs), Charles F. Browne (Artemus Ward), George Washington Harris (Sut Lovingood), Benjamin Shillaber (Mrs. Partington), Henry Wheeler Shaw (Josh Billings), and others.

   15.   Jane Curry, ed., *Samantha Rastles the Woman Question* (Champaign and Urbana: University of Illinois Press, 1983), xi. See also Curry, "Women as Subjects and Writers of Nineteenth Century American Humor" (Ph.D. diss., University of Michigan, 1975), 249. Well now, occasionally a person just can't resist quoting herself.

   16.   Nancy Walker, *Fanny Fern* (New York: Twayne Publishers, 1993), 42.

   17.   For an excellent discussion of Whitcher's work, see Linda Morris, *Women's Humor in the Age of Gentility: The Life and Works of Frances Miriam Whitcher* (Syracuse, N.Y.: Syracuse University Press, 1992). Though both

Whitcher and Holley use stereotype and caricature in their renditions of place and people, both could be viewed as part of the "local color" tradition often associated with Sarah Orne Jewett's quietly humorous sketches, Harriet Beecher Stowe's Sam Lawson stories, and other female New Englanders of the same period.

18. Among her other endearing qualities, the Widow is loquacious, vulgarly coquettish, ornery, faultfinding, backbiting, two-faced, gossipy, vain, unattractive, jealous, vindictive, gushy, and paranoid.

19. Nancy Walker, *A Very Serious Thing: Women's Humor and American Culture* (Minneapolis: University of Minnesota Press, 1988), 7–8.

Chapter One

1. Katherine Gillette Blyley, "Marietta Holley" (Ph.D. diss., University of Pittsburgh, 1936), 2–3. Blyley's work was completed within a decade of Marietta Holley's death and includes interviews with Holley contemporaries. For a thorough account of Holley's life, see Kate H. Winter's biography, *Marietta Holley: Life with "Josiah Allen's Wife"* (Syracuse, N.Y.: Syracuse University Press, 1984).

2. Blyley, 3; Winter, 13.
3. Winter, 16.
4. Winter, 19.
5. Marietta Holley, "The Story of My Life," *Watertown Daily Times*, published serially from 5 February to 9 April 1931, ch. 27. Hereafter cited as "Story," with references to chapter rather than date.
6. Winter, 20–21.
7. Winter, 15, 17, 20.
8. Winter, 17–18.
9. "Story," ch. 3.
10. "Story," ch. 1, quoted in Winter, 19.
11. Blyley, 5–6; "Story," ch. 1.
12. "Story," ch. 1.
13. Winter, 18.
14. "Story," ch. 13, quoted in Winter, 33.
15. This term is at the center of a book about antebellum women from the northeastern states who chose to remain unmarried. See Lee Chambers-Schiller, *Liberty, A Better Husband* (New Haven, Conn.: Yale University Press, 1984).
16. Winter, 33.
17. Mabel Wagnalls, "A Glimpse of Marietta Holley," *Ladies' Home Journal* (November 1903), 61.
18. "Story," ch. 2.
19. For examples, see a collection of her poems published under the name of Josiah Allen's Wife (Marietta Holley). Thus she traded on her fame as a

writer of dialect narratives to bring readers to her "more worthy" endeavors. See *Poems* (New York: Funk & Wagnalls, 1887).

20. For a detailed account of Holley's earlier poems and stories (as well as her progression in nom de plumes from Jemyma to Miss H to Marietta Hawley to Josiah Allen's Wife), see Winter, chs. 1, 2.

21. "Story," ch. 3.
22. "Story," ch. 4.
23. Winter, 64.
24. Winter, 34.
25. Marietta Holley, "How I Wrote My First Books" *Harper's Bazar* 45, no. 9 (September 1911): 405.
26. Blyley, 18, note 5.
27. Blyley, 21.
28. Sales records are not available, but in *Golden Multitudes*, Frank Luther Mott cites as best-sellers books believed to have had a total sale of 1 percent of the population of the continental United States for the decade in which it was published. In the decade 1880–89, best-sellers required a sale of at least 500,000 copies. Better-sellers are a notch below in sales but are believed to be 1 percent of the population. *Samantha at Saratoga* was listed as a better-seller for the decade.
29. To put that fee in perspective, we need to recall that this was a time of economic depression, and there was no income tax until 1913. A century later, that $14,000 fee would be equivalent to at least $500,000, depending on which economic index one consulted. Before taxes.
30. Blyley, 30; "Story," ch. 16.
31. The tale of the Dorlesky Burpy family women, for example, in *Sweet Cicely* (1887) is repeated in *Samantha on the Woman Question* (1913) with Serepta Pester as the character.

Chapter Two

1. Aileen Kraditor, *The Ideas of the Woman Suffrage Movement, 1890–1920* (New York: Anchor Books, 1971), 12–26. Two general survey accounts of the campaign for suffrage are Eleanor Flexner, *A Century of Struggle* (Cambridge, Mass.: Harvard University Press, 1959), and Andrew Sinclair, *The Emancipation of the American Woman* (New York: Harper Colophon Books, 1965), originally published as *The Better Half*. For documents pertaining to the suffrage movement, see Mari Jo Buhle and Paul Buhle, eds., *The Concise History of Woman Suffrage: Selections from the Classic Work of Stanton, Anthony, Gage, and Harper* (Urbana: University of Illinois Press, 1978). See also discussion in the introduction of Jane Curry, ed., *Samantha Rastles the Woman Question*.

2. The image of the queen bee as "executive female" is a positive one for Holley; however, it has acquired a more negative connotation a century later. A *queen bee* is seen as one who does not recognize the role of others on her

road to success and withholds assistance to other women coming along after her.
    3. "Story," ch. 4.

Chapter Three
    1. Winter, 94.
    2. Nancy Walker, "Wit, Sentimentality and the Image of Women in the Nineteenth Century," *American Studies*, XXII, no. 6 (1981): 6.
    3. *Josiah Allen's Wife as a P.A. and P. I.: Samantha at the Centennial* (Hartford: American Publishing, 1877), 468. The Widder Doodle story also appears in *The Widder Doodle's Courtship, and Other Sketches* (New York: Ogilvie, 1890).
    4. Blissful wedded partners were like "a pair of white swans floatin' down the waveless calm, bathed in silvery light, floatin' down a shinin' stream that wuz never broken by rough waves, bathed in a sunshine that wuz never darkened by a cloud." Married life was compared to "two apple blossoms hangin' together on one leafy bough on the perfumed June air, floatin' back and forth under the peaceful benediction of summer skies." Etcetery. Marietta Holley, *Samantha Among the Brethren* (New York: Funk & Wagnalls, 1890), 37–38.
    5. In "Story" Holley tells of a married minister who wonders at how Holley can portray married life so accurately given her status as a spinster. She asked him whether her portrayal was true. When he answered that it was, she says, "Many people expressed surprise that the writer being unmarried could have such knowledge of a man's nature, forgetting that every woman has a father, and usually brothers and other male relatives" (ch. 4).
    6. Walker's term.
    7. Morris, *Women's Humor in the Age of Gentility*, 13. In addition to the works of Walker and Morris, see Ann Douglas, *The Feminization of American Culture* (New York: Alfred A. Knopf, 1977), and Nina Baym, *Woman's Fiction: A Guide to Novels by and about Women in America 1820–70* (Urbana: University of Illinois Press, 1993).
    8. Morris, *Women Vernacular Humorists*, 2.
    9. *Samantha vs. Josiah, Being the Story of a Borrowed Automobile and What Came of It* (New York: Funk & Wagnalls, 1906).
    10. See Mabel Wagnall's description of Holley, ch. 1.
    11. See ch. 1, note 33, for estimates of the popularity of *Samantha at Saratoga* as reflected in sales.
    12. Winter, 6.
    13. "Story," chs. 10, 11.
    14. In *Samantha at the World's Fair* (New York: Funk & Wagnalls, 1893) Holley parodies Shakespeare when she has Samantha comment on women who, upon looking at a noble female statue, suggest petty "improve-

ments" such as elbow sleeves and bell skirts: "Some wimmen are born fools, some achieve foolishness, and some have foolishness thrust on 'em, and I guess them two had all three of 'em" (310).

15. At least Miss Flamm comes to her senses in time. Another "high flyer of fashion," similarly bound and corseted, is unable to move to save her child's life when a vase falls on her head. It was reported in the paper as "a mysterious dispensation of Providence." Samantha says that Providence was slandered (381–84).

16. The narrative is sprinkled with periodic examples of Ardelia's verse. One verse from "Stanzas on a Mineral Spring" will suffice as illustration. See chapter 2 for an example of Betsey Bobbet's poetry in "A Song."

> Oh! Waters that doth bubble up and spout
> Oh, didst thou bubble down insted of up,
> Thou couldest not with all thy minerals get out
> We could not then arise and drink thee in a cup. (193)

Chapter Four

1. Eleanor Flexner, *Century of Struggle: The Woman's Rights Movement in the United States* (New York: Atheneum, 1973), 181.
2. Sara M. Evans, *Born for Liberty* (New York: Free Press, 1989), 126.
3. Flexner, 182.
4. Quoted in Evans (126), who quotes from Barbara Epstein, *The Politics of Domesticity* (Middletown, Conn.: Wesleyan University Press, 1981), 96.
5. "Story," ch. 5.
6. "Story," ch. 1.
7. "Story," ch. 8.
8. "Story," ch. 3.
9. *Samantha in Europe* (New York: Funk & Wagnalls, 1893), *My Wayward Pardner* (Hartford: American Publishing, 1880), *Samantha at the World's Fair* (New York: Funk & Wagnalls, 1893), and *Samantha vs. Josiah* (New York: Funk & Wagnalls, 1906).
10. "How I Wrote," 404–5.
11. "Story," ch. 19.
12. "Story," ch. 15.
13. The Freedman's Bureau (1865–72) was the popular name for the U.S. Bureau of Refugees, Freedmen, and Abandoned Lands, established by Congress to provide practical aid to 4 million newly freed black Americans in their transition from slavery to freedom. Through the bureau, hospitals were built, direct medical assistance given, and rations distributed. The most notable contribution, however, was probably in the field of education where more than 1,000 schools were built for blacks and $400,000 was spent to establish teacher-training institutions. The major black colleges were either founded by or received financial help from the bureau.

14. In an 1894 lecture entitled "The Lesson of the Hour," Frederick Douglass decried the idea of colonization to Africa, saying that it was not out of love but out of hate for the Negro.

15. The Fourteenth Amendment to the U.S. Constitution was ratified on 9 July 1868. Although the principal purposed of this amendment was to grant citizenship to former slaves, it also introduced the word *male* into the Constitution for the first time in a way that was used specifically to exclude females from voting. Section 2 of the amendment proposes a penalty for states that deny "the right to vote at any election" to "any of the male inhabitants of such state being twenty-one years of age. . . ." Many in the women's rights movement who had ardently supported abolition felt betrayed by the insertion of the word *male* in this amendment. It was another 50 years (1920) before the Nineteenth Amendment granted women the right to vote.

16. The Southern Question in the later suffrage movement involved issues of states' rights and maintenance of white supremacy.

17. Because he "has the intellect for it and the pans" (188).

18. "Story," ch. 27.

19. Blyley, 28. Blyley was able to interview Holley's longtime gardener and others who provided firsthand accounts of her daily habits.

20. Though Holley has no Jewish characters in her works, she occasionally resorts to stereotype by describing someone as being "rich as a Jew." And in her way of bringing the lofty down to the common level, Samantha refers to His Holiness of the Catholic Church as Mr. Pope and decries the practice of keeping church members in ignorance. See chapter 2.

21. In *Samantha Among the Colored Folks* Samantha uses the same language in describing blacks as she had used for the Old Testament prophets: "They were burnt at the stake; they were sawed asunder; they were destitute, afflicted, tormented" (132). She also notes that the "black Africans" had no reporters of their own to tell their stories; therefore, the full histories were unread by the public. Thus Holley uses religious imagery to link the histories of women and people of color because white, male writers have done the recording.

22. Sometimes Josiah has a fence to fix, a cow to milk, a mare to feed, and so on. Whatever the excuse, he extricated himself from situations in which Samantha clearly has the logical upper hand and preserves his illusion that he has had the last word.

23. See discussion, ch. 2.

Chapter Five

1. Samantha maintains that punishment should be for reforming criminals and not for the "malicious enjoyment to the punishers. . . . And that is why I never could believe that chokin folks to death was the way to reform 'em and make better citizens of 'em" (553). One chapter tells the story of the poor

man who steals codfish and onions to feed his consumptive wife. The townspeople call for harsh punishment but brush off news that $150,000 had been stolen from the public treasury by claiming it a "little case of fraud," a mere "deficit in accounts" (133).

Samantha uses the example of schoolyard squabbling to castigate the notion of war. "Why . . . you'd whip a lot of school children that would go to settlin' their quarrels with their jack knives; you'd make them leave it out to the teacher, or the trustees, or somebody. . . . Children ort to grow wiser as they grow older instead of foolisher; it haint a mite handsomer in grown folks than it is in children" (401).

2. Thomas Francis O'Donnell, "The Regional Fiction of Upstate New York" (Ph.D. diss., Syracuse University, 1957), note 238.

3. "Story," ch. 16.

4. The dedication echoes the words of Bertha Honore Palmer, chairwoman of the Board of Lady Managers for the Woman's Building, when she spoke at the opening ceremonies. In "The Story of My Life" Holley notes that she met Mrs. Potter Palmer when she visited the Fair. Palmer's comment: "Even more important than the discovery of Columbus, which we are gathered together to celebrate, is the fact that the General Government has just discovered woman." She added that had it not been for Queen Isabella, Columbus would never have set sail. Samantha, too, is taken with Queen Isabella and emphasizes her role in America's discovery. For a comprehensive account with illustrations of the Woman's Building and its exhibits from more than 30 countries, see Jeanne M. Weimann, *The Fair Woman* (Chicago: Academy Press, 1981). An earlier Weimann article, "A Temple to Women's Genius: The Woman's Building of 1893," appeared in *Chicago History* (spring 1977), 23–33.

5. Refers to Susan B. Anthony, who in 1872 led a group of Rochester, New York, women to the polls, was arrested, found guilty, and fined $1. On principle she refused to pay the fine but was prevented by a technicality from appealing her case to a higher court.

6. Winter, 126.

7. Winter, 127.

8. Or in most cases the innocent children of the arrogant rich.

9. In *Samantha Among the Colored Folks* the age of consent was "over seven" (see 235–41).

10. See ch. 1. Also Winter discusses Holley's relationship with May and her habit of taking in "stray boys" who needed guidance and/or had gotten into some trouble.

11. Given Holley's own juggling of child rearing and writing for about 10 years with May and her comments about her commitment to her art cited in an earlier chapter, it is interesting that Samantha lectures this poet about the necessity of not choosing two masters: "If one loved Art well enough to wed it and leave father and mother for its sake, well and good, but after choosin' love

and home and children, how necessary and beautiful it wuz to tend to them first of all, and then pay attention to Art afterwards" (58).

12. See Robert A. Smith, *A Social History of the Bicycle* (New York: McGraw-Hill, 1972).

13. Approximately 10,000 women marched on Pennsylvania Avenue that day. The women had been given a permit to march, but inadequate police protection allowed an angry mob to break it up. In England, the women's Social and Political Union had been formed in 1903. Known as the Militant Suffragettes, they waged a campaign for the vote that eventually went beyond petitions, speeches, and peaceful demonstrations to include violent tactics such as rock-throwing, window-smashing, arson, and bombings. For a documentary account of their struggle, see Midge Mackensie, *Shoulder to Shoulder* (New York: n.p., 1975).

14. With the exception of the posthumously published autobiography many years later.

15. Winter, 145–46.

16. The Eighteenth Amendment to the U.S. Constitution prohibiting the manufacture, sale, and transportation of liquor was ratified in 1919.

Chapter Six

1. Winter, 68. She cites the local paper, *Jefferson County Journal*, and Clara Barton's diary as sources.

2. Cited in Blyley, 17.

3. Blyley, 16–17, and "Story," ch. 8.

4. "Story," ch. 8.

5. Blyley, 17. For accounts of Burgess and *Vim*, see Morris, *Women Vernacular Humorists*, ch. 5, entitled "Wolves in Sheep's Clothing: Four Male Humorists Who Masqueraded as Women," and Alfred Habegger, *Gender, Fantasy, and Realism in American Literature* (New York: Columbia University Press, 1982), 166–68. Habegger quotes from a review of *Vim* by William Dean Howells in which Howells claims the play is a triumph of realistic humor. Clearly not a fan of Holley's, Habegger suggests that the reason Howells liked *Vim* better than the Holley books was that the play eliminated didacticism. "Burgess took the one important humorous character that functioned as an auxiliary to a decidedly self-righteous women's movement and transmuted her into a type associated with local color and petticoat humor. Not until she was impersonated by a man could Samantha take it easy and become 'homicidally funny.'" Copies of programs, posters, reviews, clippings, scrapbooks, and portraits of Neil Burgess and *Vim* are included in the archives of the Billy Rose Theatre Collection of the New York Public Library.

6. Morris, *Women Vernacular Humorists*, 267. She contrasts Holley's original words with Burgess's version in a few key speeches, showing that

Burgess (1) focuses on the men, not the women, (2) often lets Josiah have the last word, (3) parodies the domestic details he appropriates from Holley, and (4) changes critical phrasings and language for his antifeminist ends.

7. Winter, 147; information based on accounts in the *Watertown Daily Times*.

8. Walter Blair and Hamlin Hill, *America's Humor: From Poor Richard to Doonesbury* (New York: Oxford University Press, 1978), 496.

9. To his credit, Hill admitted as much after seeing a performance at the University of Tel Aviv during a symposium commemorating the sesquicentennial anniversary of Mark Twain's birth. During the question period, I was asked how I had discovered Samantha. Citing Blair's *Horse Sense in American Humor*, which had first steered me toward Holley, I quoted, lamentably, from the then-recent anthology and allowed as how of course I didn't know which of them had written that particular passage. With his wife beside him, red-faced with laughter throughout the show, and a room full of delighted people making the acquaintance of the unschooled rustic, Hill hollered from the back of the room, "Walter did it! Walter did it!"

10. "How I Wrote," 404.

11. *World's Fair*, 256. In *My Opinions* Samantha tries to barter in a New York City store that doesn't recognize that mode of economic exchange. With a sense of her own notoriety and characteristic modesty, she offers her socks and mittens without revealing her identity. "I wasn't goin' to have 'em go, jest because one of the first wimmen of the day knit 'em" (351).

Periodically Samantha met people who referred to her books. In *My Opinions* Dr. Mary Walker says, "Oh! . . . I have read your eloquent orations on wimmen havin' a right." At a garden party in Calcutta in *Around the World*, a woman acknowledges that she "had hearn on me, so she said, and she said she had laughed some when she read my books, and had cried too, and I sez, 'I hope you didn't cry because you felt obleeged to read 'em, or somebody made you. . . .'" (241–42).

12. *National Cyclopaedia of American Biography*, vol. 9, 278.

13. Ellis Parker Butler, "The Uniqueness of Marietta Holley," *Mark Twain Journal* (spring–summer 1958): 11.

14. Quoted in Winter, 64; from *Woman's Journal*, Boston (22 June 1878).

15. Charlotte Templin, "Attention and Neglect: The Reputations of Marietta Holley and Mark Twain," in manuscript (therefore no page numbers will be cited).

16. Given this assessment, it is somehow fitting that *Samantha Among the Brethren* is one of the few Holley books to have been reprinted. It was part of a series of reprints of works on the tradition of American Protestantism. *Samantha Among the Brethren* is also the source of the selection made for the *Heath Anthology of American Literature* (Lexington, Mass.: D. C. Heath, 1990).

17. Both quotations are found in Walker, "Wit, Sentimentality and the

Image of Women in the Nineteenth Century," 22, note 39. Ashwell's comment is in *Native American Humor*, 947, xiii. The Hollis essay is included in Louis D. Rubin, ed., *The Comic Imagination in American Literature* (New Brunswick, N.J.: Rutgers University Press, 1973). Some historians no doubt believe they are also citizens. See discussion of performance history for a perception of Holley's interest to modern-day citizens.

Thomas Francis O'Donnell calls Holley an "ugly duckling offspring of the 'damned mob of scribbling females' of the 1850s." To describe her he uses phrases such as "relentless point of view," "ill-placed condescension," and "ponderous moralizing." Apparently by way of compliment, he says: "shallow, tiresome, and provincial as she often is in the Samantha books, Marietta Holley is never hypocritical or insincere." "The Regional Fiction of Upstate New York" (Ph.D. diss., Syracuse University, 1957), 232–45.

18. Alfred Habegger, *Gender, Fantasy, and Realism in American Literature* (New York: Columbia University Press, 1982), 164–67.

19. See also Elizabeth Ammons, "Men of Color, Women, and Uppity Art at the Turn of the Century," *American Literary Realism 1870–1910* 23, no. 3 (1991): 14–24; and Paul Lauter, in "Race and Gender in the Shaping of the American Literary Canon: A Case Study from the Twenties," *Feminist Studies* 9 (fall 1983): 435–63. They claim that "the racial and sexual character of the American literary canon has resulted from a series of deliberate choices by scholars and other powerful cultural arbiters" (Ammons, 18). Professionalization of the study of American literature worked to exclude women. It is neither historical accident nor unapproachable genius that has for the nineteenth and most of the twentieth century institutionalized a nearly all white, male literary canon.

20. Elisha Bliss and the American Publishing Company published and True Williams illustrated books for both authors. According to Kate Winter, Williams told Holley that Twain was jealous of her, a declaration she dismissed as "babble" coming from the lips of an oft-inebriated illustrator. Twain wrote a review of *My Wayward Pardner*, in which he gave a backhanded compliment that he liked it better than its predecessor. She indicated in her autobiography that she had his books on her shelves but hadn't read any except *Tom Sawyer* all the way through because she found them too sharply satirical.

Whether Holley ever met Twain is unclear. On the one hand, she liked to tell of meeting Twain at a reception in his honor in New York City. When she was announced in the reception line, he obviously did not recognize her. She claimed that she whispered "Samantha," whereupon he heartily replied, "Samantha! I've always loved you." On the other hand, in her autobiography she denied meeting him, although she remembered the banquet in his honor (Winter, 135).

21. Linda Morris notes that Holley's writing career was unusually long for a humorist; in fact, for the good of her literary reputation, she says, it was too long. "Had her career been a shorter one, ending in 1887 with the publication of her fifth and most popular novel, *Samantha at Saratoga*, it is likely that today we would count her among the major humorists of the nineteenth centu-

ry" (*Women Vernacular Humorists*, 150). I would argue for a date in the early 1890s after both *Samantha Among the Brethren* and *Samantha on the Race Problem* had been published. Also, the reason Holley's work has been ignored seems more connected to her advocacy of a feminist point of view than to the number of rerun books she wrote in the last half of her career.

22. Templin also discusses the importance of their differing personal styles and acquaintances. Unlike the timid Holley, Samuel Clemens was an avid self-promoter who created the public personality of Mark Twain, engaged audiences on the lecture circuit, used his trademark white suit as an identifying prop, and enjoyed the friendship of the influential William Dean Howells.

23. Walker, *A Very Serious Thing*, 170–71.

24. Fred Lewis Pattee, "On the Rating of Mark Twain," in *Essays on Mark Twain 1910–1980*, ed. Louis J. Budd (Boston: G. K. Hall, 1983), 82.

25. See ch. 1, note 9, for a list of articles published about Holley. In the *Heath Anthology of American Literature* Holley is included in a section called "Issues and Visions in Post–Civil War America" along with W. E. B. DuBois, Charlotte Perkins Gilman, Henry Adams, and others.

26. Ann Douglas, *The Feminization of American Culture* (New York: Alfred A. Knopf, 1977), 11.

27. Morris's term, *Women Vernacular Humorists*.

28. *Samantha on the Race Problem*, 326–33.

Selected Bibliography

PRIMARY SOURCES

Novels

Around the World with Josiah Allen's Wife. New York: Dillingham, 1905.
Josiah Allen on the Woman Question. New York: Revell, 1914.
Josiah Allen's Wife as a P. A. and P. I.: Samantha at the Centennial. Hartford: American Publishing, 1877.
My Opinions and Betsey Bobbet's. Hartford: American Publishing, 1873.
My Wayward Pardner, or, My Trials with Josiah, America, the Widow Bump, and Etcetery. Hartford: American Publishing, 1880.
Samantha Among the Brethren. New York: Funk & Wagnalls, 1890.
Samantha at Coney Island and a Thousand Other Islands. New York: Christian Herald, 1911.
Samantha at Saratoga, or, Flirtin' with Fashion. Philadelphia: Hubbard, 1887.
Samantha at the St. Louis Exposition. New York: Dillingham, 1904.
Samantha at the World's Fair. New York: Funk & Wagnalls, 1893.
Samantha in Europe. New York: Funk & Wagnalls, 1895.
Samantha on Children's Rights. New York: Dillingham, 1909.
Samantha on the Race Problem. New York: Dodd, Mead, 1892. (Republished as *Samantha Among the Colored Folks,* 1894.)
Samantha on the Woman Question. New York: Revell, 1913.
Samantha vs. Josiah, Being the Story of a Borrowed Automobile and What Came of It. New York: Funk & Wagnalls, 1906.
Sweet Cicely, or, Josiah Allen as Politician. New York: Funk & Wagnalls, 1885.

Stories, Plays, Poems, and Autobiography

Betsey Bobbet: A Drama. Adams, N.Y.: W. J. Allen, 1880.
"How I Wrote My First Books," *Harper's Bazar* 45, no. 9 (September 1911), 404–5.
Josiah's Alarm, and Abel Perry's Funeral. Philadelphia: Lippincott, 1895.
Josiah's Secret: A Play. Watertown, N.Y.: Hungerford-Holbrook, 1910.
Lament of the Mormon Wife, The. Hartford: American Publishing, 1880.
Miss Jones's Quilting and Other Stories. New York: Ogilvie, 1887.
Miss Richards' Boy and Other Stories. Hartford: American Publishing, 1883.
Poems. New York: Funk & Wagnalls, 1887.
Story of My Life, The. Watertown, N.Y.: Times Publishing, 1931.

Tirzah Ann's Summer Trip, and Other Sketches. New York: Lupton, 1892.
Widder Doodle's Courtship, and Other Sketches, The. New York: Ogilvie, 1890.

SECONDARY SOURCES

Books, Parts of Books, and Articles

Blair, Walter. *Horse Sense in American Humor.* Chicago: University of Chicago Press, 1942. Blair devotes about 10 pages to Holley and places her firmly in this tradition of American humor.

Blyley, Katherine Gillette. "Marietta Holley." Ph.D. diss., University of Pittsburgh, 1936. Completed within a decade of Holley's death, this thesis offers sound insights and invaluable resources, including information based on interviews with Holley contemporaries. Among these was Lew Hoxie, who served as Holley's handyman and typist for many years.

Curry, Jane. "Women as Subjects and Writers of Nineteenth Century American Humor," Ph.D. diss., University of Michigan, 1975. This thesis has a chapter each on Holley and Whitcher but also looks at how male humorists treated female characters. A revised version of the Holley chapter was published as "Samantha 'Rastles' the Woman Question," *Journal of Popular Culture.* VIII, no. 4 (spring 1975), 805–24.

———, ed. *Samantha Rastles the Woman Question.* Urbana: University of Illinois Press, 1983. This anthology of selections reprinted from Holley's works is organized generally by topics within the "woman question" as addressed by Samantha. An audiotape by the same title, with selections performed by Curry, was also issued by the University of Illinois Press in 1983.

Morris, Linda. *Women's Humor in the Age of Gentility: The Life and Works of Frances Miriam Whitcher.* Syracuse, N.Y.: Syracuse University Press, 1992. An excellent study of the cultural restrictions of the genteel tradition on women and of Whitcher, whose work predated and influenced Holley's.

———. *Women Vernacular Humorists in Nineteenth-Century America: Ann Stephens, Frances Whitcher, and Marietta Holley.* New York: Garland Publishing, 1988. This fine analysis discusses characteristics of the vernacular tradition, then offers critical insights on how these authors used and/or transformed it for their own ends.

Wagnalls, Mabel. "A Glimpse of Marietta Holley." *Ladies' Home Journal* 20 (November 1903): 61. An affectionate account of her interview with Holley, which includes Holley's account of why she chose her pseudonym.

Walker, Nancy. "Wit, Sentimentality, and the Image of Women in the Nineteenth Century." *American Studies*, XXII, no. 2 (1981): 5–22. Holley is discussed as a clearly feminist writer attacking the sentimental tradition through humor.

———. *A Very Serious Thing: Women's Humor and American Culture.* Minneapolis: University of Minnesota Press, 1988. A groundbreaking work in criticism of women and American humor, this book discusses both overt and covert ways in which women's humor typically subverts cultural gender norms and expectations.

———and Zita Dressner, eds. *Redressing the Balance: American Women's Literary Humor from Colonial Times to the 1980s.* Jackson: University Press of Mississippi, 1988. This anthology reprints excerpts from approximately 50 women writers working in various forms—poetry, fiction, nonfiction, diaries, newspaper columns—ranging from colonial traveler Sarah Kemble Knight to lesbian comic Gail Sausser.

Winter, Kate. *Marietta Holley: Life with "Josiah Allen's Wife."* Syracuse, N.Y.: Syracuse University Press, 1984. The first full-length biography of Holley, this thorough, well-researched volume was written by a native of Holley's North Country region of New York State.

Index

abolition, 2, 12, 40, 49
Adventures of Huckleberry Finn, The. See Huck Finn
age of consent, 75, 79, 102n9
American Publishing Company, 6, 105n20
America's Humor: From Poor Richard to Doonesbury, 85
Anne of the Island, 86
Anthony, Susan B., 8, 17, 24, 71n5, 102n5
antisuffrage (*see also* she auntys), 17, 91
Arthur, Chester, 48
Aswell, James, 88
"Attention and Neglect: The Reputations of Marietta Holley and Mark Twain," 87

Baptists, 2, 23, 57, 58
Barton, Clara, 9, 10, 81
beautiful weakness and simplicity, as theme, 27, 33
Beecher, Henry Ward, 8
Betsey Bobbet, xiii, 4, 6, 14–16, 19, 21–22, 29–32, 81, 85
Betsey Bobbet Clubs, xiii, 81–82
bicycle, 77
Billings, Josh, 6
black Africans, 27, 48, 52, 101n21
Blaine, James G., 48
Blair, Senator Henry, 8, 41
Blair, Walter, xiii, 85, 88
Bliss, Elisha, 6, 7, 8, 105n20
Bonnie View (residence), 9–11
Brown, Antoinette, 8
Burgess, Neil, xiii, 83–84, 103n5,6
Butler, Ellis Parker, 87

cacography, xvi, 85
canon, 88, 91, 105n19
capitalism, 74
Carleton, Will, 9
Centennial Exposition, 7, 68–70, 72

Chicago World's Fair, 68, 70, 72, 86
children's rights, 10–11, 25, 68, 76–77, 91
church, women and, 40, 57–67
Claverack College, 8, 84
Clemens, Samuel. *See* Twain, Mark
Cleveland, President Grover, 9
clinging vine, 18, 31
Colfax, Schuyler, 8
colonization/colonialism, 55–56, 74, 75
Columbia, 69, 71, 72
Columbian Exposition, 68, 70
comic reversal, 90–91
common sense, xiv–xvi, 22, 33, 39, 82
"County Fair, The," 83
Creation Searchin' Society, 79–80
Critic, The, xiii
Curry, Jane: as performer, 84–85; quoted, xvi

Declaration of Independence, 66
dialect, xiv–xvi, 5–7, 16, 30, 57, 85
Dorlesky Burpy (fictitious), 45–48, 78
double standard, 20, 25, 42, 60–62, 76
Douglas, Ann, 90, 92
Douglass, Frederick, 8, 101n14
Down East tradition, xiv–xv
Downing Papers, The, 18
Dunne, Peter Finley, xv

Eaton, S. Homer, 82
Eighteenth Amendment, 11
equal pay, 20, 26, 78, 91
Equal Rights Amendment, 78, 91

fashion, 5, 20, 23, 25, 35–39, 49
feminist/feminism, xiv, xvi–xviii, 6, 69, 81, 84–85, 87, 89, 105–6n21
Feminization of American Culture, The, 90
Fern, Fanny (pseudonym), 32
Flack, Alonso, 8
foremothers (4 mothers), xviii, 21, 36, 47, 60, 81, 85

111

Fourteenth Amendment, 56, 101n15
Foxe's Book of Martyrs, 13, 58
free love, 20, 24–25
freedman's schools, 54, 100n13

gender spheres. *See* public/private spheres
General Conference, Methodist, 63
genteel tradition/gentility, 14–15, 22, 31–39, 74, 75, 77, 90
Grant, Ulysses S., 17, 25, 50, 69
Greeley, Horace, 17, 23, 25–29, 33, 65

Habegger, Alfred, 88, 103n5
Hamilton, Gail (pseudonym), 32
Harper's Bazar, 13
Harte, Brett, 6
Heath Anthology of American Literature, 90
Hill, Hamlin, 85, 88, 104n9
history, treatment of women in, 59–60, 101n21
Holbrook, Hal, 84
Holley, Marietta: as adoptive parent, 10; childhood of, 1–4; compared to Mark Twain, xiii–xiv, 88–89, 92; death of, 11; described, 1, 9; early writing years, 4–7; education, 2–3; film adaptations of works of, 84; financial situation of, 9, 98n29; first travels, 8–9; illness, 3, 10–11; literary reputation of, 86–92; popularity of, xiii–xiv; pseudonyms of, 4–5, 12, 31, 77, 98n20; religion/spirituality of, 2, 3; on women's indirect influence, 60

FICTION
Around the World with Josiah Allen's Wife, 73–76
Josiah Allen on the Woman Question, 10, 11, 76, 80
Josiah Allen's Wife as a P. A. and P. I.: Samantha at the Centennial, 7, 16, 31, 34, 35, 37, 50, 61, 68, 69, 70, 75, 87
Miss Jones's Quilting and Other Stories, 31
Miss Richards' Boy, 9, 31

My Opinions and Betsey Bobbet's, 2, 6, 9, 12–30, 31, 42, 52, 58, 65, 68, 70, 77, 81, 89
My Wayward Pardner, 7, 10, 31, 33, 58
Samantha Among the Brethren, 10, 16, 32, 34, 62–67, 87
Samantha at Coney Island and a Thousand Other Islands, 77
Samantha at Saratoga, or, Flirtin' with Fashion, 9, 31, 33, 36–39
Samantha at the St. Louis Exposition, 10, 19, 70, 72, 73
Samantha at the World's Fair, 9, 10, 37, 69–71
Samantha in Europe, 10, 73, 76
Samantha on the Race Problem, 10, 49, 53–57, 68
Samantha on the Woman Question, 12, 68, 76, 77–78
Samantha vs. Josiah, Being the Story of a Borrowed Automobile and What Came of It, 34, 58, 60, 76, 87
Sweet Cicely, or, Josiah Allen as a Politician, 9, 42–49, 50, 51, 58, 60, 62, 71, 78, 87

POEMS, ESSAYS, PLAY, AUTOBIOGRAPHY
Betsey Bobbet: A Drama, 7, 16, 83, 84
"Fourth of July in Jonesville," 5
"Gypsy and I," 6
"How I Wrote My First Books," 30, 49, 81, 82
Lament of the Mormon Wife, The, 7, 31, 58
"Phair and Phalse," 6
"Piety," 5
Poems, 9
"Story of My Life, The," 2, 6, 41
"Welcome to Summer," 4

Holley, Henry, 5
Holley, John, 1–3
Holley, Mary Taber, 1, 3, 7
Holley, Sylphina, 3, 7, 9, 11
Hollis, C. Carroll, 88
Holmes, Oliver Wendell, 5
Home Journal, 7

Index

Hooker, Isabella Beecher, 24
horse sense, xiii–xiv, 11, 16, 85
Horse Sense in American Humor, xiii, 88
housekeeping metaphor, 13, 41
Hoxie, Lew, 9, 10
Huck Finn, xvi, 14, 18, 89
Hungerford, General Solon, 8

Ideas of Woman Suffrage, The, 17
imperialism, 51, 68, 75
Indians, 48, 50–51, 69
Innocents Abroad, The, 73

Jack Downing (fictitious), xv, 18
Jefferson County Journal, 4, 5
Josiah Allen (fictitious), 4, 6, 12–13, 19–20, 23, 34, 36, 38–39, 42, 54–55, 57, 62–66, 68, 70–76, 79–80, 82, 84, 86, 90
Josiah Allen's Wife (pseudonym), xiii, 5, 6, 7, 12, 27, 31, 77, 85, 86, 98n20
juries, 72

Kirkland, Caroline, 32
Kraditor, Aileen, 17

language, xiv–xvi, 16, 21, 32–33, 47, 53, 55, 58, 62–63, 65–66, 85, 91, 101n21
Letters of a Woman Homesteader, 86
local color, xiv–xv, 96–97n17
Lyceum, 2, 8

malapropisms, xvi, xviii, 16, 18
marriage, 4, 16, 32, 43, 58–59, 80, 99n4,5
"megumness" (moderation), 17, 23, 36, 38, 61, 69, 80, 82
Methodist Church (Methodists), 18, 23, 25, 58, 63, 65, 92
Militant Suffragettes, 79–80, 103n13
Montgomery, L. M., 86
Mormons, 58–59
Morris, Linda, xiv–xvi, xviii, 33, 83–84

National Cyclopaedia of American Biography, 87
National Woman Suffrage Association, 8
Native Americans, 50

nativism/ethnic stereotype, 26, 50, 52, 101n20
nature, 5, 21, 28, 43, 44, 47–48, 55, 69
Newman, John C., 9
Nineteenth Amendment, 11, 80
nom de plume. *See* Holley, Marietta, pseudonyms of
Nye, Bill, 87

Ogilvie, J. S., 31
Old Testament prophets, wives of, 36, 57, 59–60, 92, 101n21

Partington, Mrs. (fictitious), xviii, 18
Pattee, Fred Louis, 89
Peace Commission, 48, 51
pedestal argument, 19
performance history, xiii, 81–86
Peterson's Magazine, 5, 6, 13
Phillips, Wendell, 8
poll, 19–20, 22, 26
polygamy, 31, 58–59
preachers, women as, 28–29, 65
public/private spheres, xvii–xviii, 15–16, 19, 22–23, 26–29, 33, 43–44, 47–48, 60, 65, 78, 90–91

queen bees, 28, 98–99n2
Queen Isabella, 102n4
Queen Victoria ("Widder Albert"), 17, 27

race/racism, 40, 49–57, 69, 100–101n13–16
Reconstruction, 53, 54, 56
Redressing the Balance: American Women's Literary Humor From Colonial Times to the 1980s, 90

sales records, 9, 98n28,29
Samantha Allen (fictitious) (*see also* Josiah Allen's Wife): creation of, 5–6; described, 13, 91; on "megum" approach to life, 23; on own fame, 86; on sentiment, 14–15; as wise innocent, 18; on women's foibles, 21
Sanborn, Kate, xiii

Saratoga Springs, 7, 36, 82
Schlafly, Phyllis, 78
Seneca Falls, 17, 69
sentimental female poet, 31, 38
sentimental tradition, xvi, 31–39, 89, 91
Shaver, May, 10, 11, 76
she auntys, 78–79
Sherman, General, 8
Shillaber, Benjamin, xviii, 18
Sigourney, Mrs. L. H., 5
Simon Slimpsey (fictitious), 16
slavery, 12, 49, 52–53, 89
Smith, Seba, xv, 18
socialist utopia, 74
Southworth, E. D. E. N., 31
speaking in public, women, 20, 28, 65
spiritualism, 3, 57–58, 68, 76
Stanton, Elizabeth Cady, 17, 24, 26
statues, 37–38, 43, 51, 71–72, 99n14
Stewart, Elinor Pruitt, 86
Stowe, Harriet Beecher, 8
suffrage. *See* woman suffrage

Taylor, Bayard, 8
temperance, 2, 8, 11, 20, 26, 40–49, 57, 68, 74, 78, 80, 87
Templin, Charlotte, 87, 88–89
Thomas Jefferson Allen (fictitious), 13, 25, 42, 76, 83
thought-children, books as, 10, 82
Tirzah Ann Allen (fictitious), 13, 25, 33, 42, 76, 83
travel motif, 7, 18, 30, 31, 36, 68, 70, 72–76, 91
Twain, Mark, xiii, xiv, 6, 8, 14, 18, 41, 73, 84, 86, 87, 88–90, 92, 105n20, 106n22

unpaid labor, women as, 64

vernacular, xiv–xvi, xviii, 5, 16, 81, 90–91
Very Serious Thing, A, xvi, xvii

Vim, 83, 84

Wagnalls, Mabel, 5, 6, 9
Walker, Mary, 17, 23, 24, 104n11
Walker, Nancy, xvi–xvii, 32, 89
war, 68, 72, 74, 75, 101–2n1
Warner, Charles Dudley, 6
Warner, Susan, 31
Washington, Booker T., 50
Watertown Daily Times, 2, 11
WCTU. *See* Women's Christian Temperance Union
Whitcher, Frances, xv–xvi, 21, 32, 33, 83
white slavery, 56, 75–76
"Widow and the Elder, The," 83
Widow Bedott (fictitious), xv, xvi, 83, 97n18
wife beating, 43, 45, 46, 47
Willard, Frances, 8, 40–41, 63
Williams, True, 41, 105n20
Wilson, Woodrow, 79
Winter, Kate, 4, 5, 10, 80
wise innocent, xiv, 18
Wit of Women, The, xiii
woman suffrage, 2, 8, 11, 17, 19–22, 24, 26, 40–41, 44, 47–48, 51–52, 56, 63, 68–69, 78–80, 89, 91
Woman's Building, 71–72, 86, 102n4
Woman's Pavilion, 69, 72
women: economic dependence on men of, 16, 26, 33, 58, 64, 67; as preachers, 28–29, 65
Women Vernacular Humorists in Nineteenth-Century America, xiv
Women's Christian Temperance Union, 8, 40, 41, 47, 61
Women's Humor in the Age of Gentility, xv, xvi, 33
women's rights, 12–30, 35, 47, 53, 69, 77–80, 82, 87, 91
Woodhull, Victoria, 17, 24–25

xenophobia, 51

The Author

A native Hoosier, Jane Curry is a storyteller, performer, and recovering academic. She received her B.A. from Hanover College in Indiana and her A.M. and Ph.D. from the University of Michigan. After teaching English and American studies at Lafayette College, Curry left the academic world to ride steamboats, write, and educate through performance.

Winner of the 1983 Minnesota Independent Scholar of the Year Award, Curry is the author of *The River's in My Blood: Riverboat Pilots Tell Their Stories* (1983) and editor of an anthology of selections from Marietta Holley's works, *Samantha Rastles the Woman Question* (1983). She toured for nine seasons with the Minnesota Chautauqua and performs nationally and internationally with three solo shows she has written: *Samantha Rastles the Woman Question*, *Just Say Know: Educating Females for the 21st Century*, and *Nice Girls Don't Sweat*.

Curry lives in Minneapolis, Minnesota, and is currently working on her latest performance piece, *Miz Wizard's Science Secrets*.

The Editor

Nancy A. Walker is Director of Women's Studies and Professor of English at Vanderbilt University. A native of Louisiana, she received her B.A. from Louisiana State University and her M.A. from Tulane University. After receiving her Ph.D. from Kent State University in 1971, she taught American literature, American Studies, and Women's Studies at Stephens College, where she also served as Assistant to the President and Chair of the Department of Languages and Literature.

A specialist in American women writers, Walker is the author of *A Very Serious Thing: Women's Humor and American Culture* (1988) and *Feminist Alternatives: Irony and Fantasy in the Contemporary Novel by Women* (1990), which won the first annual Eudora Welty Prize. She has published numerous articles in such journals as *American Quarterly, Tulsa Studies in Women's Literature, American Literature,* and *American Literary Realism,* and several essays on women's autobiography. With Zita Dresner, she edited *Redressing the Balance: American Women's Literary Humor from the Colonial Period to the 1980s* (1988).

Walker currently serves as general editor for the period 1800–1914 for Twayne's United States Authors Series and is editing a new critical edition of Kate Chopin's *The Awakening* for St. Martin's Press.

OHIO UNIVERSITY LIBRARY
Please return this book as soon as you have
finished with it in order to avoid a fine it must